MW01617915

LEONARD NIMOY

SECRET SELVES

MASS MoCA
NORTH ADAMS, MASSACHUSETTS

TABLE OF CONTENTS

FOREWORD

Even before reading Leonard Nimoy's artist statement, with its reference to Aristophanes, my first reaction to this series of photographs shot in 2007 was that the images were strangely classical: beneath the staged, sometimes whimsical, occasionally inexplicable costumes, and behind the sometimes haunting overabundance of id, they possess a stately, architectonic quality, their subjects rigorously contained in columnar geometries and tightly restricted spaces. The image of caryatids — columns that cross-dress as figural sculpture—spring to mind.

Most of the photographs' subjects — carefully directed and photographed by Nimoy — define their alternative selves in a moment of purposeful repose. Then, having locked these figures in sharp-edged, posed stasis, it is as if Nimoy conspired to withhold from these "hidden selves" all hope of actual physical grounding: he grants them no permanent respite in this world of ours. Instead, the characters float against a marble white, nearly shadowless background, the presence of their costumed bodies suspended in a series of frieze-like spaces, caught forever in the abstract. This equivocation between the subject's plastic, almost sculptural presence, and its literal groundlessness, makes for compelling work, all the more so since those are our neighbors caught there. Here in the Berkshires we recognize some of these people, which is all the more eerie and intriguing.

But I confess that even before seeing the photographs, I dove into the B-roll... the remarkable "making of" DVD that captures Nimoy in the gentle act of directing his collaborators before the lens. This short documentary captures a wide swathe of human interaction: we witness a range of personalities confronting one of the world's most recognizable celebrities, and then being warmly engaged by someone else entirely, the photographer Leonard Nimoy, even as each of the sitters is cajoled into entering his or her own alternative self. Nimoy's human empathy and fine hand as art director, laced with his dauntingly precise technical control and more than a little manipulation, make for an alluring series of photographic transactions.

I join our staff in thanking Leonard Nimoy and Rich Michelson for allowing us to show this engaging body of work for the first time. The fact that it brings to our museum some of the most interesting characters from a neighboring town, widely celebrated for its interesting characters, makes the project all the richer. And a personal thanks to Susan Nimoy, through whom we got to know Mr. Nimoy's photography.

Visitors to the museum probably noted something else interesting about this show: in addition to generous support from Bonnie Moss, the show was sponsored by hundreds of people of all ages and backgrounds, instead of the one or two big corporations or foundations whose names we're used to seeing on gallery walls. This was an experiment with a new kind of art support in the age of social networking. The response was delightful — people truly want to help keep art on the walls — and proves that there are vast reservoirs of goodwill for the arts, so long as we make it affordable, participatory, direct, and fun.

— Joseph C. Thompson, Director

At Plato's Symposium around 400 B.C. Aristophanes posited a theory which could explain human angst. Humans, he suggested, were at one time double-sided creatures having two heads, four arms and four legs. In this form they became powerful and arrogant, angering the gods. Zeus was sent to solve the problem; this he did by cleaving everyone in two with a huge sword. Since then humans have been searching for the other, lost part of themselves in order to feel complete again. As Aristophanes put it, "...human nature was originally one and we were whole..."

Secret Selves is an exploration of the concept of the lost or hidden or fantasy self.

—*Leonard Nimoy*

SCOTT — CHILDREN'S BOOK ILLUSTRATOR

I play music for preschoolers... but that's a bunch of screaming kids, not a bunch of screaming girls.

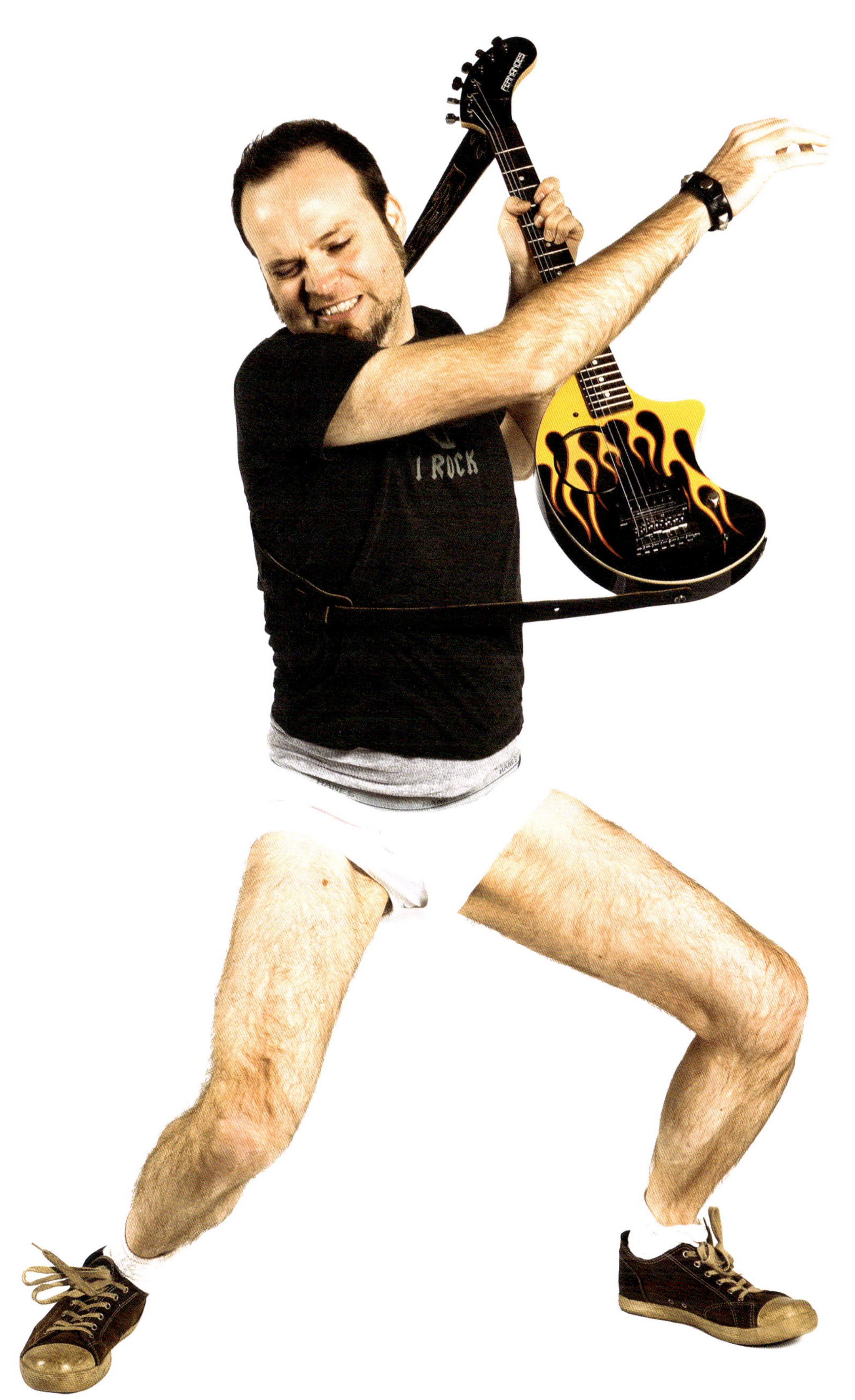
I ROCK

AMANDA — WAITRESS/COSMETOLOGIST

My father was a pastor so… I had to be mature. So now is my time… to play.

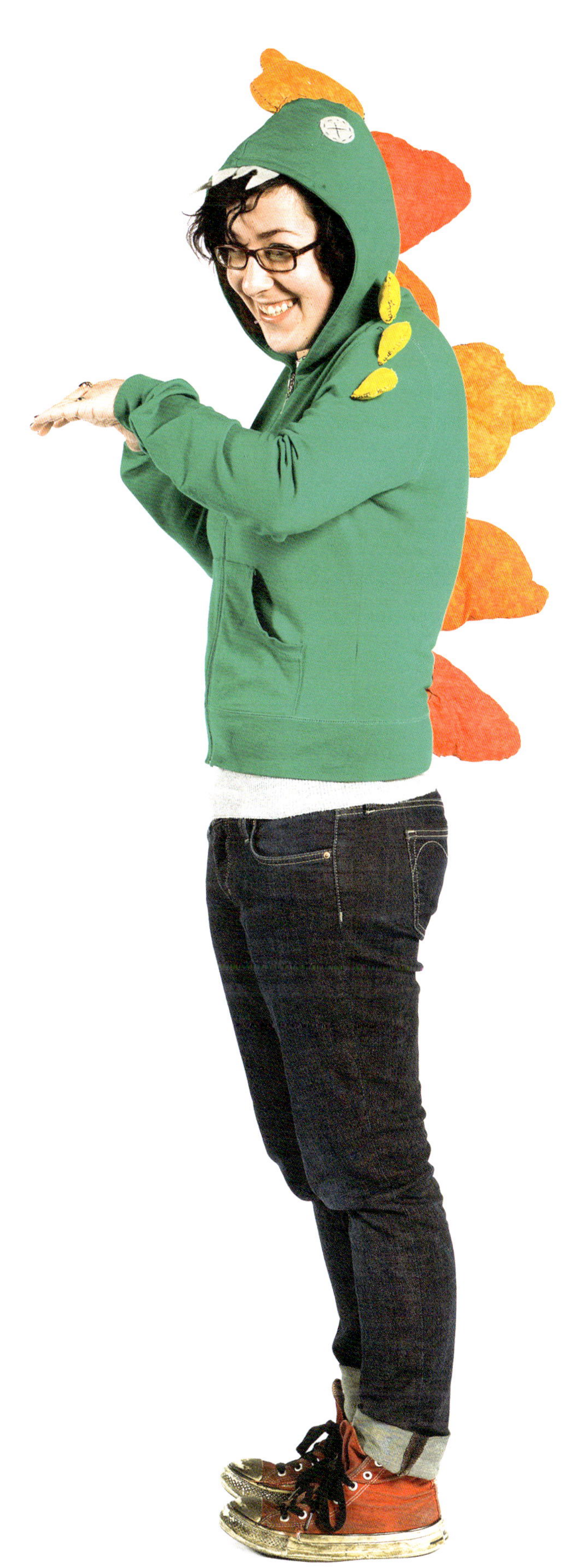

JAMES — NEWSPAPER ARTS EDITOR

I plan to retire into a career as a mad scientist. I believe it is only madness of purpose that will serve me well.

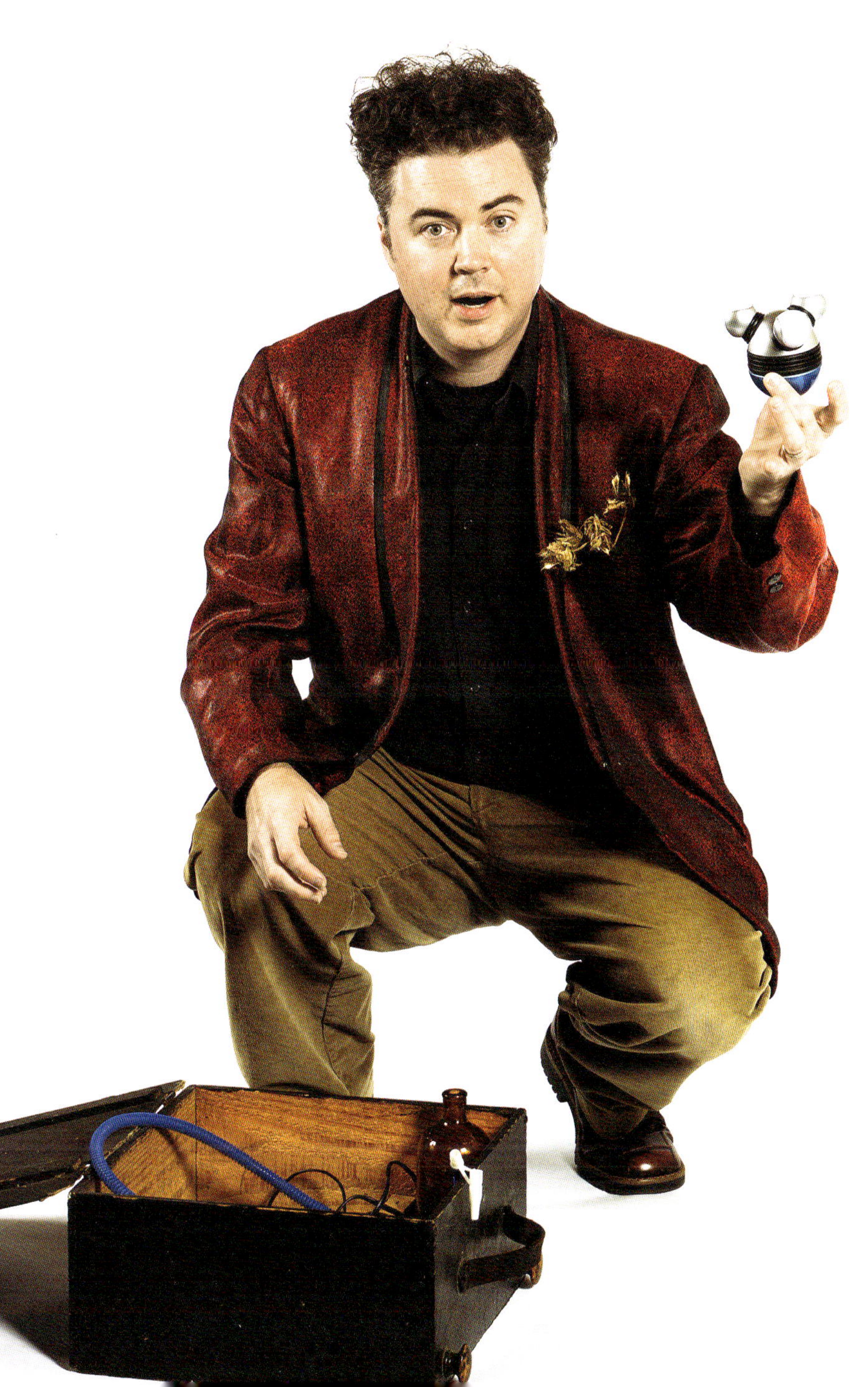

EMILY — RETREAT CENTER DIRECTOR

I'm becoming a sheep farmer. Right now I'm a total fraud: once you meet sheep farmers you see how much there is to learn.

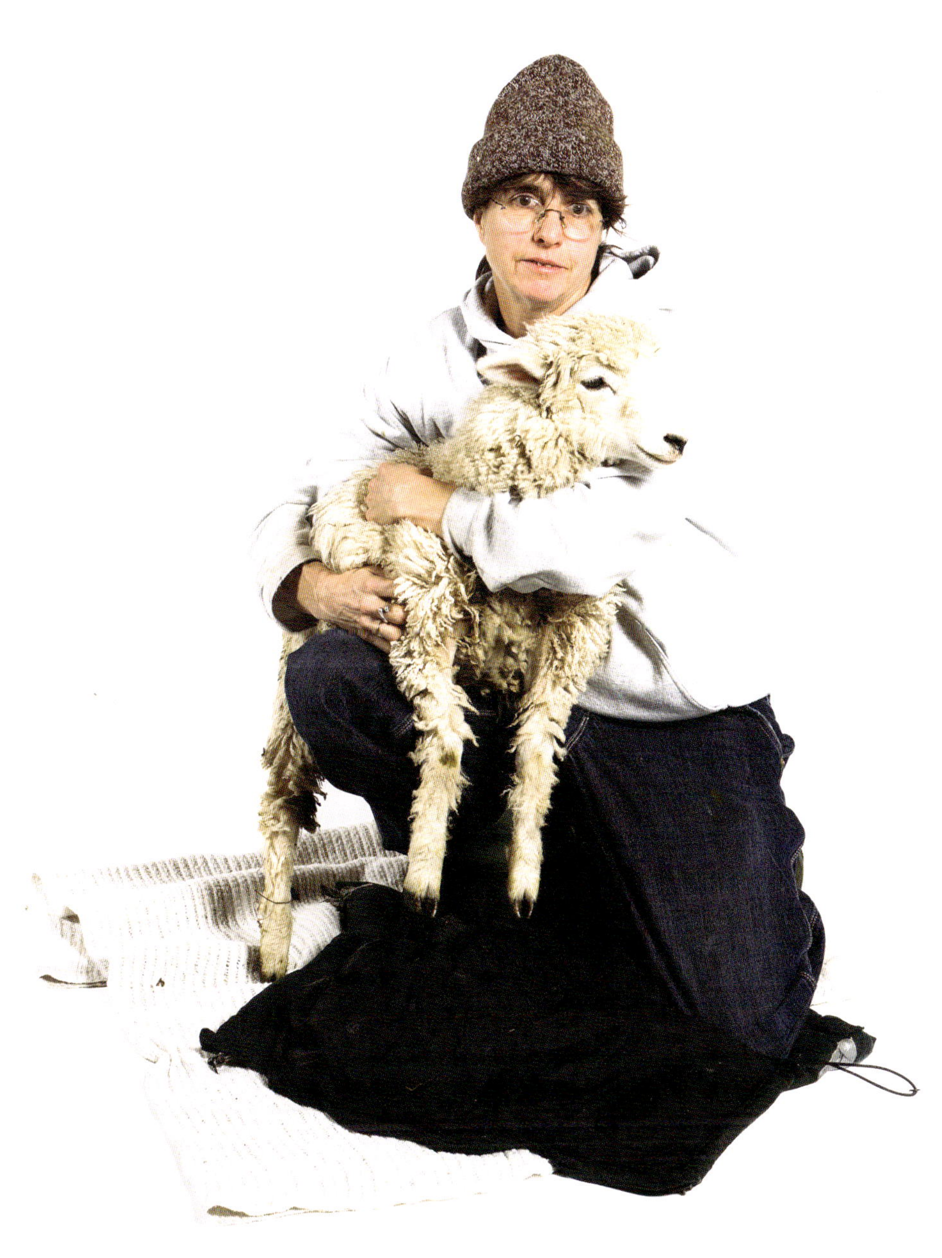

NANCY — AESTHETICIAN

Life is paint, and I am both the canvas and the artist.

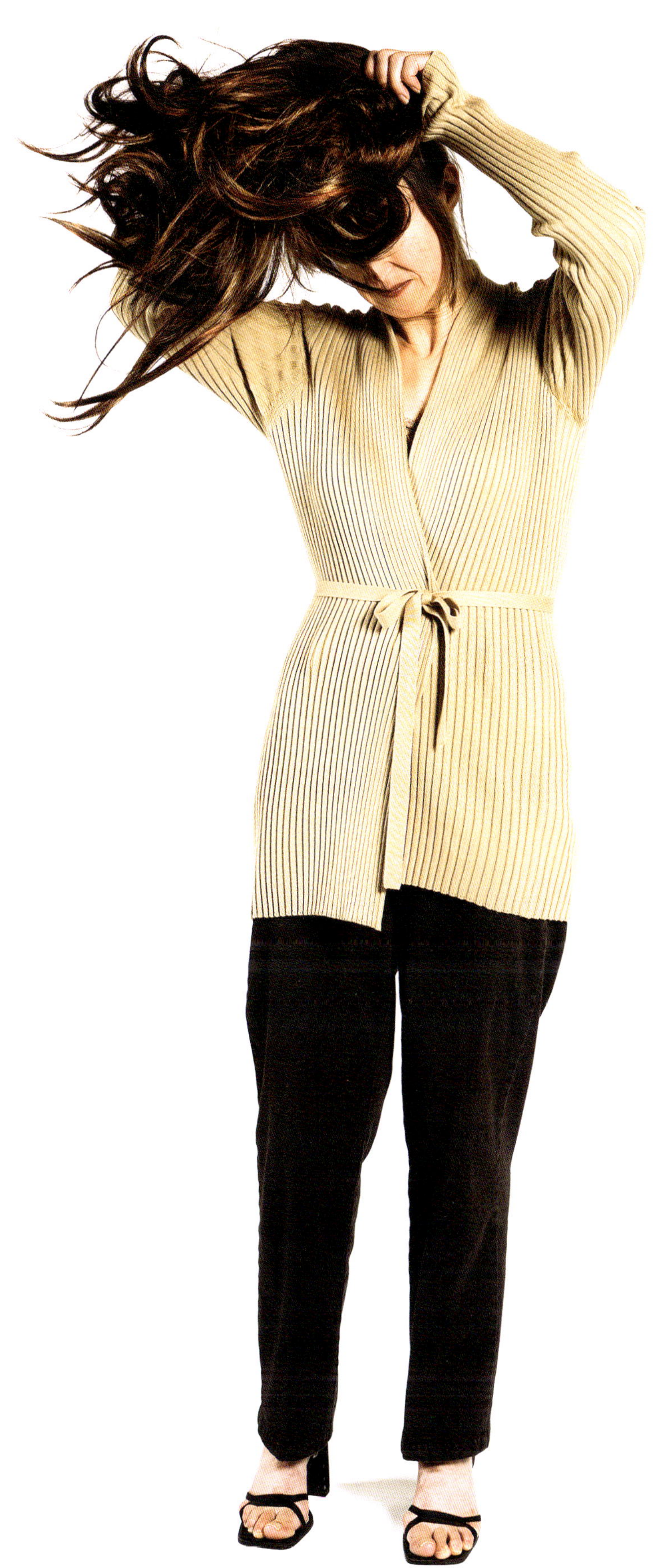

VALDORISE — TOY COMPANY EMPLOYEE

I've always called myself the secret whore, a character based on what I'd do if I could.

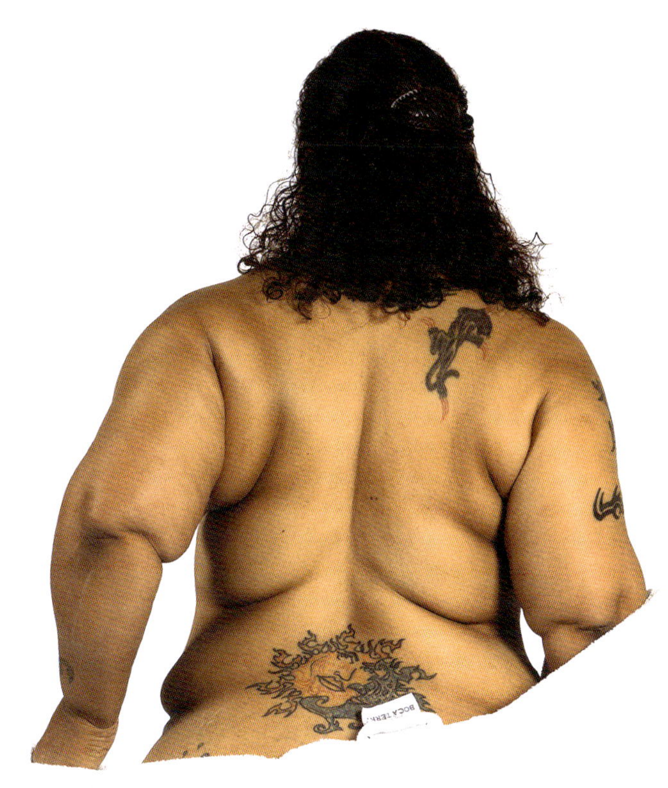

LISA — DIRECTOR OF COMMUNICATION

My own story comes from all the stories I've heard.

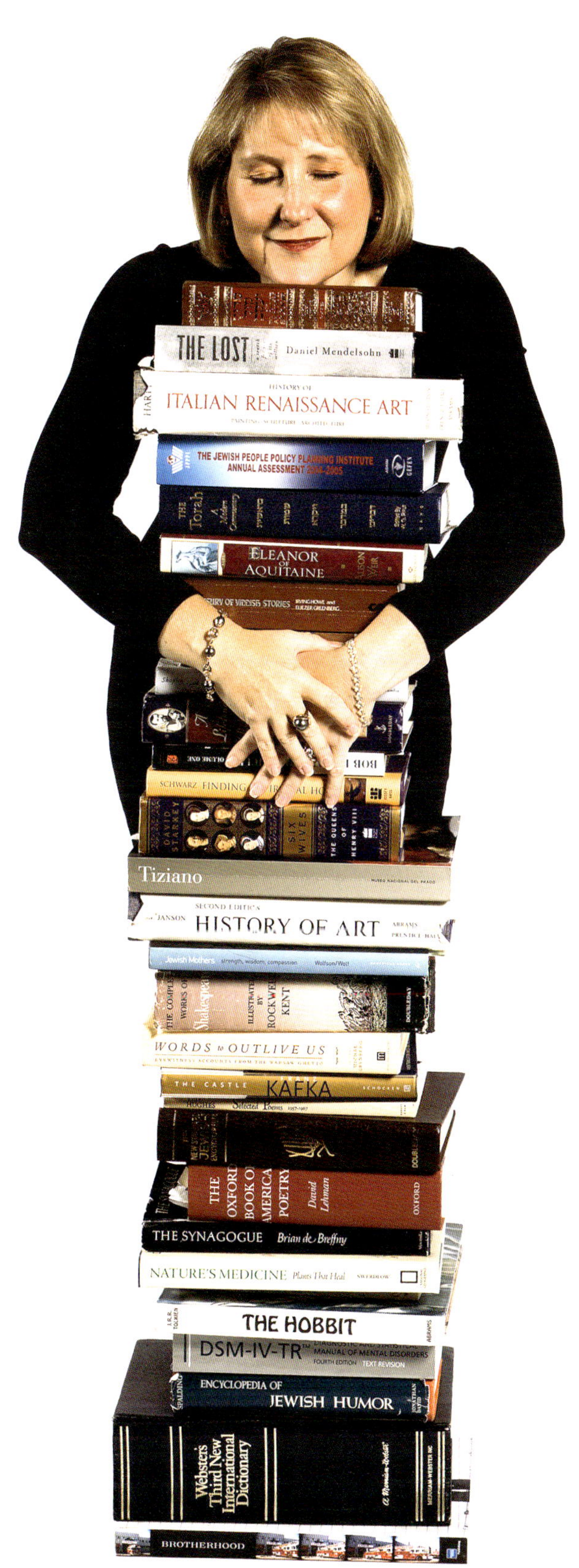

THE LOST
Daniel Mendelsohn
HISTORY OF
ITALIAN RENAISSANCE ART
THE JEWISH PEOPLE POLICY PLANNING INSTITUTE
ANNUAL ASSESSMENT 2004-2005
GEFEN
THE Torah A Modern Commentary
ELEANOR OF AQUITAINE
ALISON WEIR
IRVING HOWE and ELIEZER GREENBERG
SCHWARZ
DAVID STARKEY
SIX WIVES
THE QUEENS OF HENRY VIII
Tiziano
MUSEO NACIONAL DEL PRADO
SECOND EDITION
JANSON
HISTORY OF ART
ABRAMS
PRENTICE HALL
Jewish Mothers
ILLUSTRATED BY ROCKWELL KENT
DOUBLEDAY
WORDS to OUTLIVE US
THE CASTLE
KAFKA
SCHOCKEN
Selected Poems
DOUBLEDAY
David Lehman
OXFORD
THE SYNAGOGUE
Brian de Breffny
NATURE'S MEDICINE
Plants That Heal
THE HOBBIT
DSM-IV-TR
MANUAL OF MENTAL DISORDERS
FOURTH EDITION
TEXT REVISION
ENCYCLOPEDIA OF
JEWISH HUMOR
Webster's Third New International Dictionary
A Merriam-Webster
BROTHERHOOD

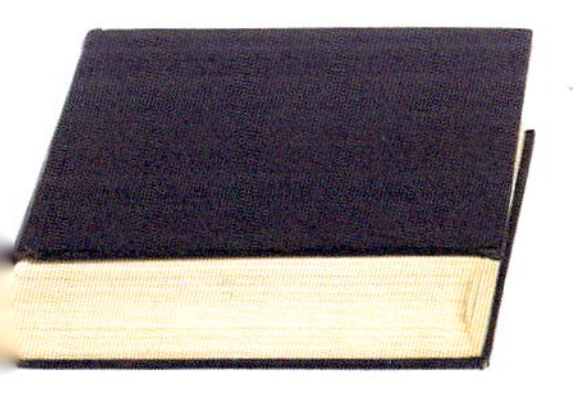

NATALIE — FOSTER CARE MOTHER

I want to show that I still have a lot of female in me.

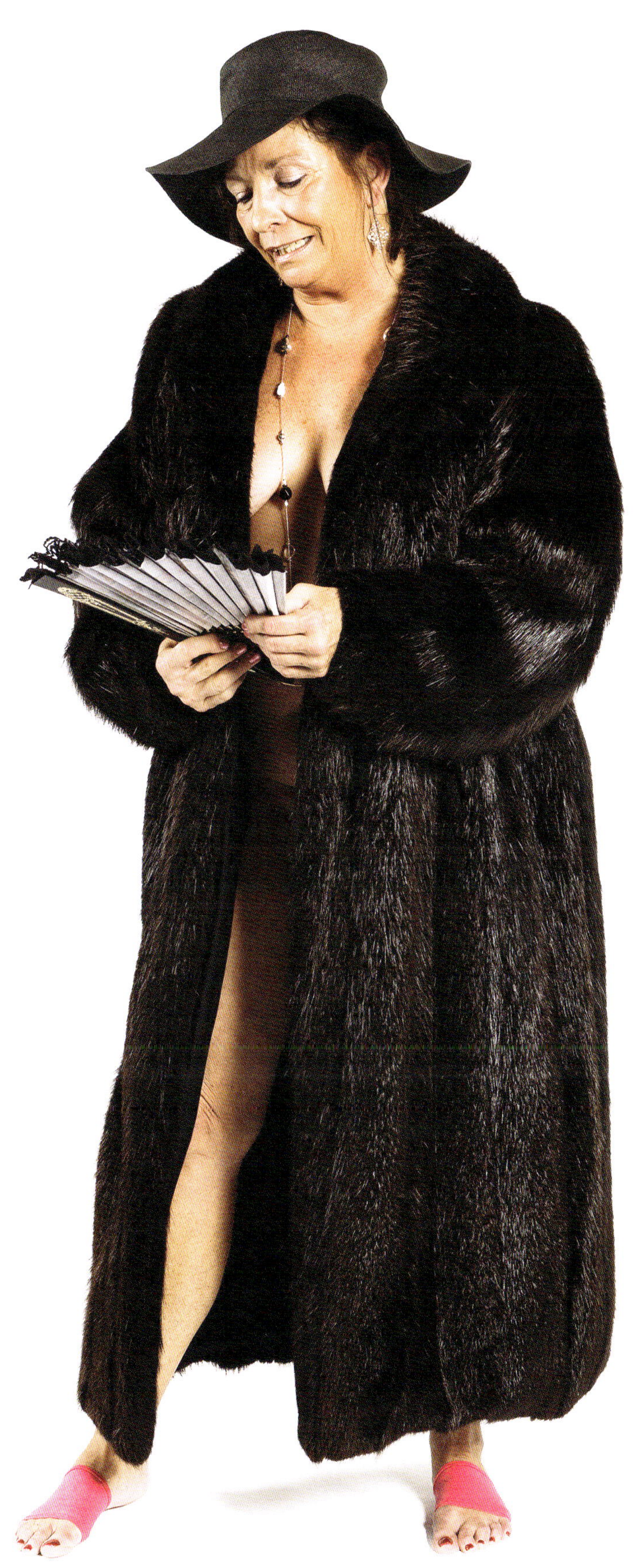

KATHLEEN — PSYCHOTHERAPIST

I usually wear pretty clothes, but when I go to buy a car or something the inner pit bull comes out.

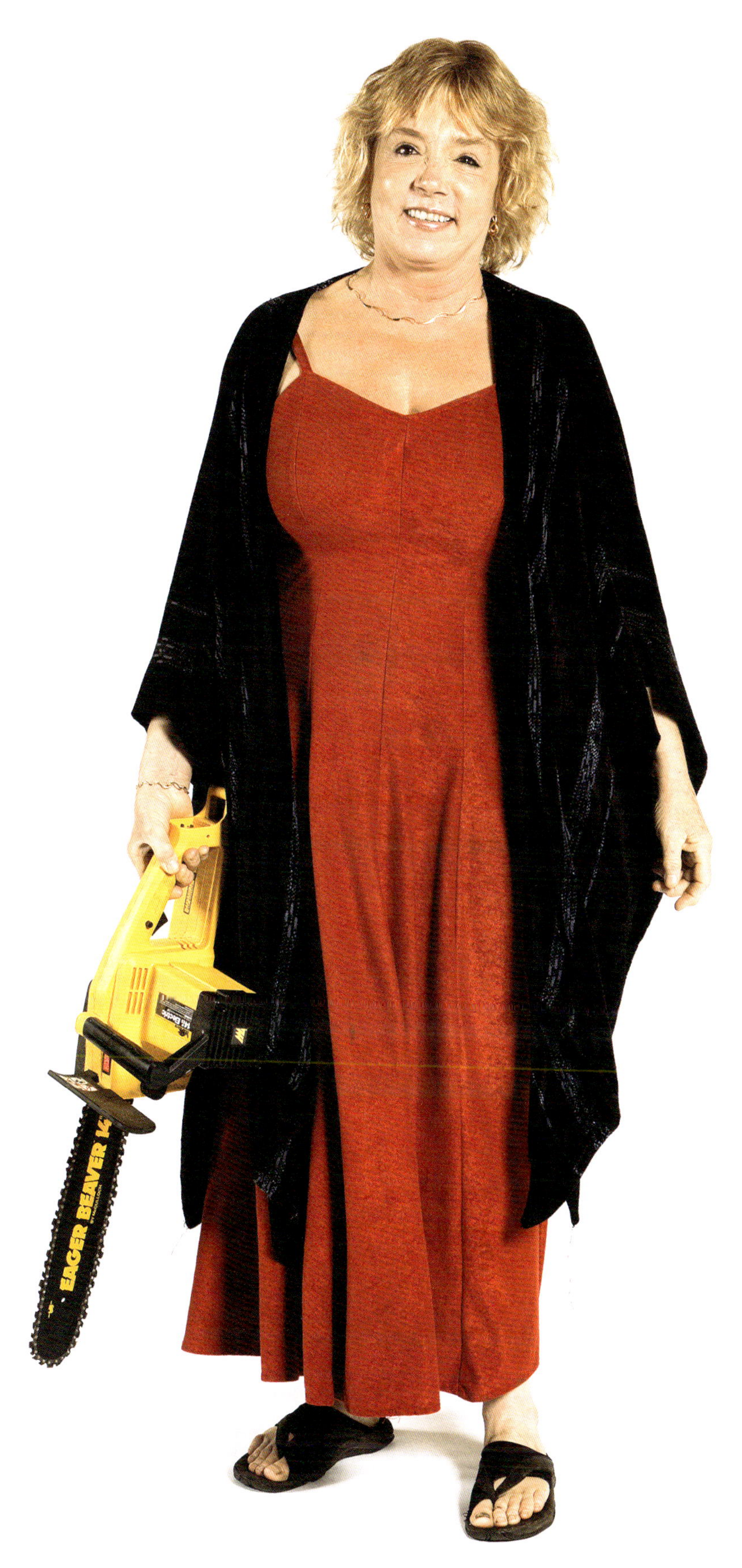
EAGER BEAVER

MATT — PAINTER OF AMERICANS WHO HAVE WITNESSED WAR

I would aspire to be a force of nature, a simple and pure avatar of the Earth.

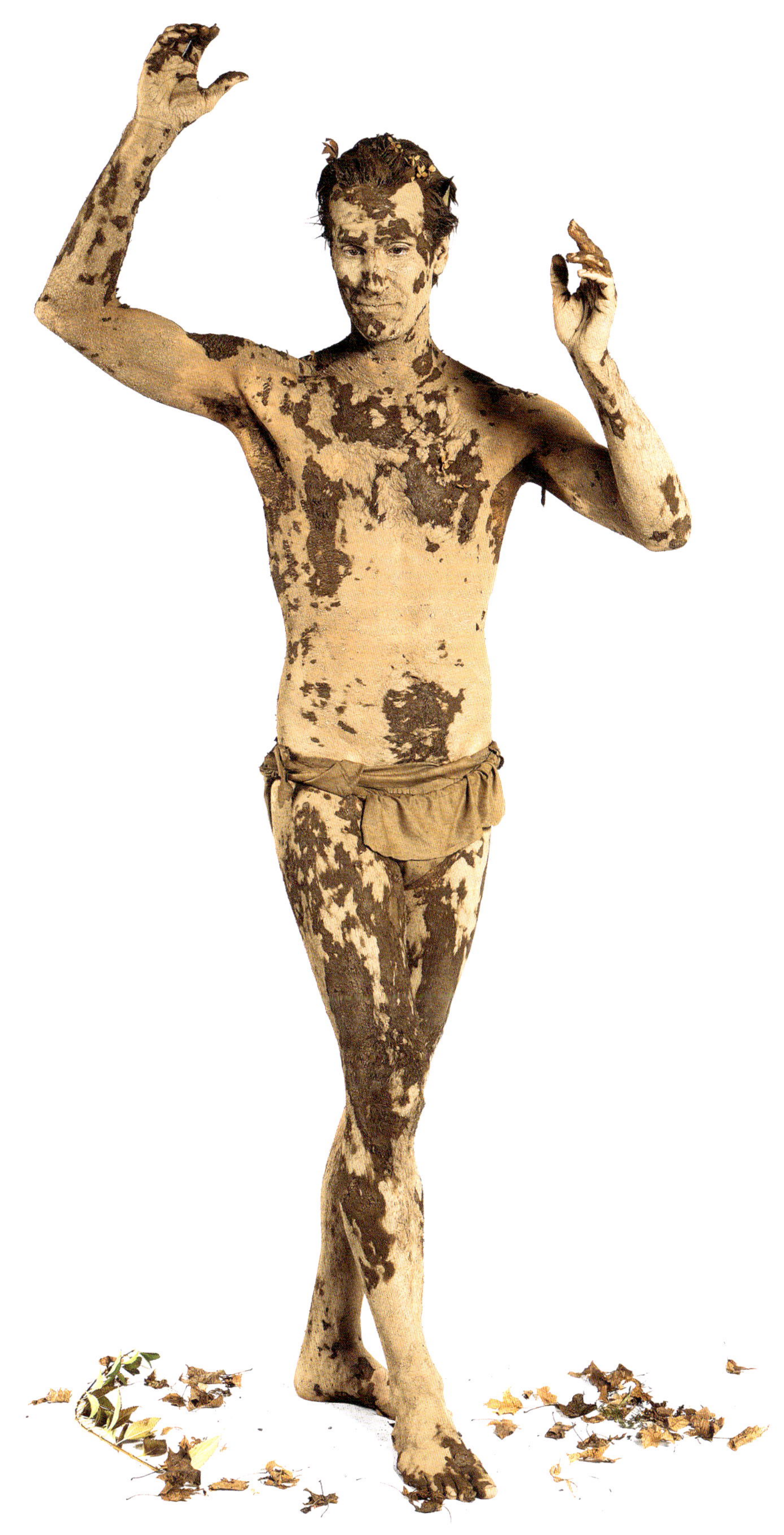

MICHAEL — PUBLIC RELATIONS MARKETING

I want to look tougher than I do.

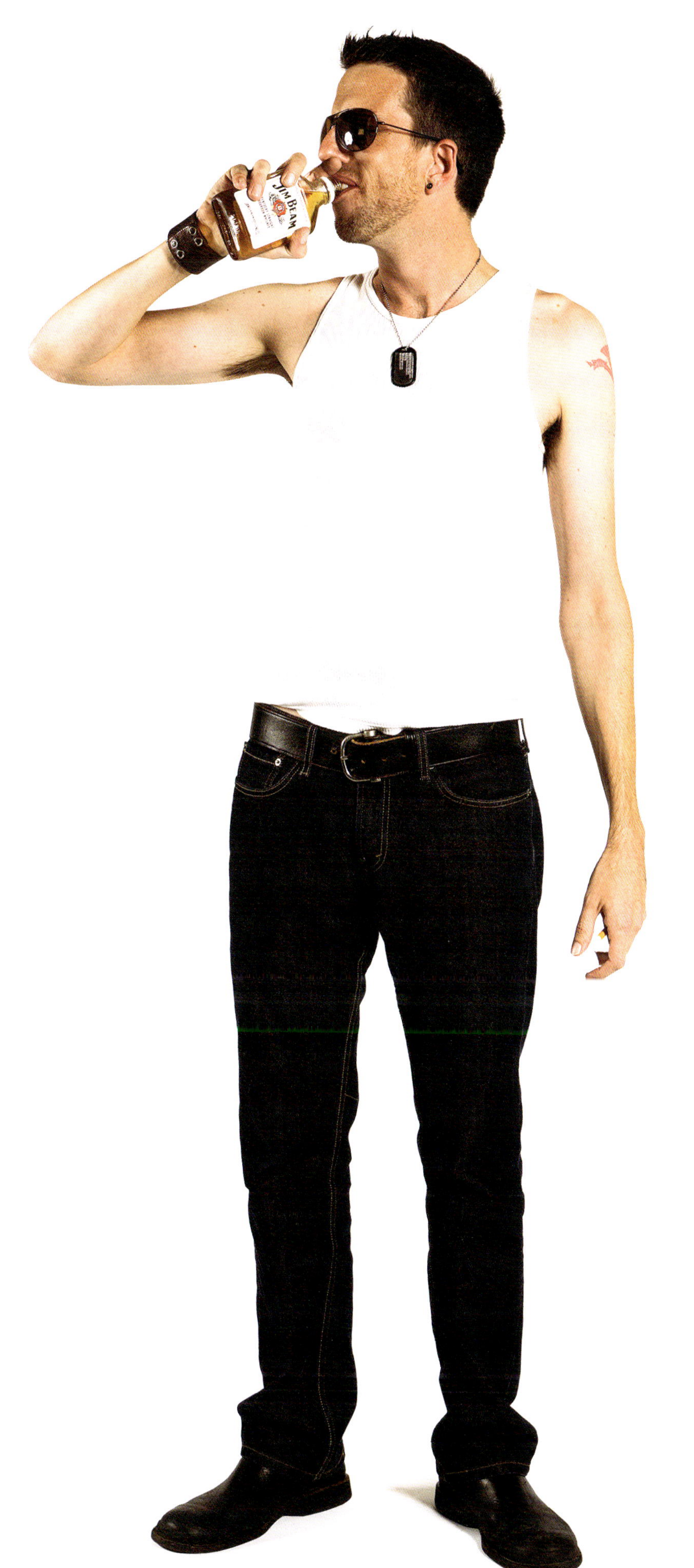
JIM BEAM

JOSEPH — U.S. NAVY

I was born and got this Superman cape and a green bear that I take with me everywhere.

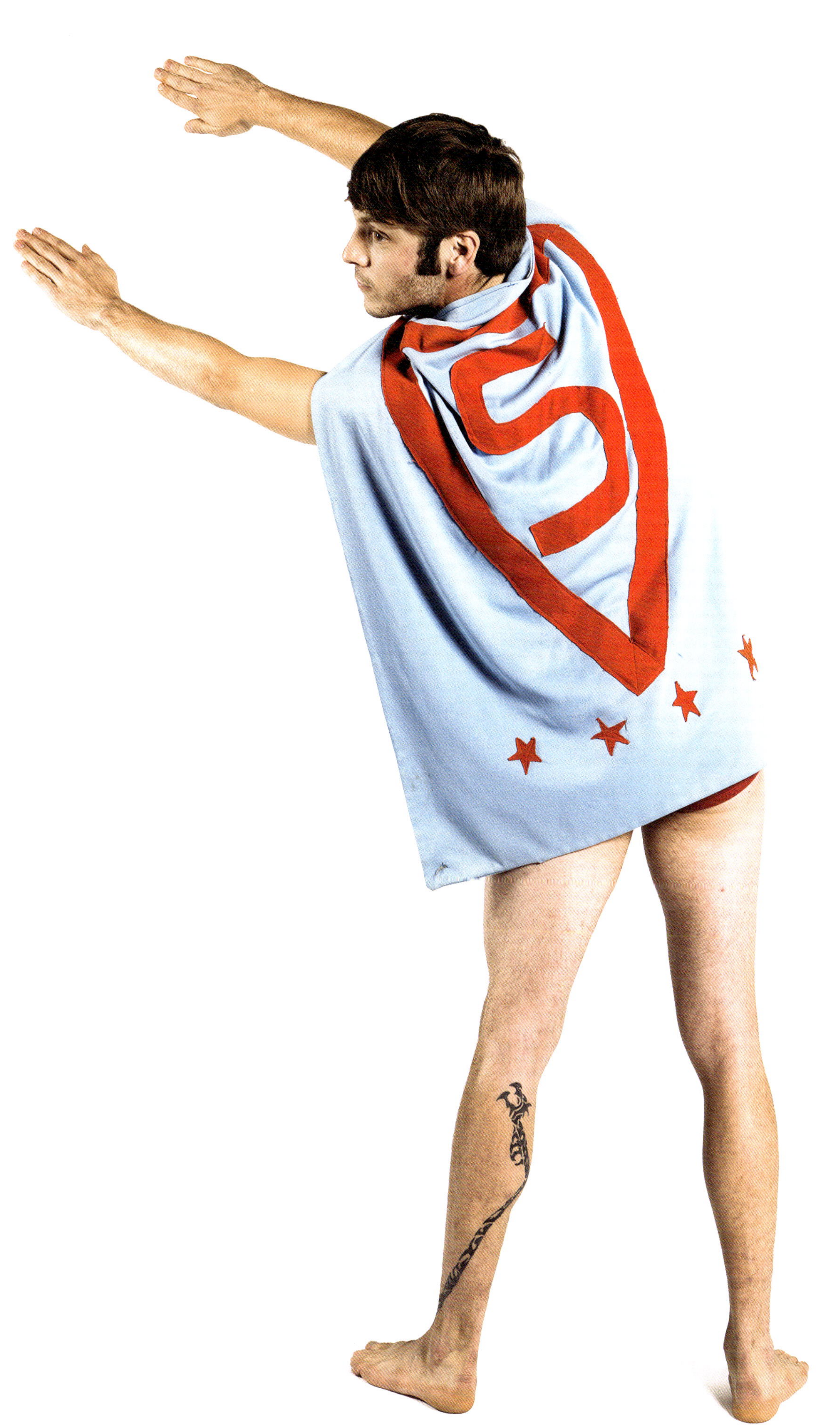

TAMMY — EX-MARINE/TEACHER FOR BEHAVIORALLY CHALLENGED CHILDREN

I live life as Clark Kent, but I'd rather be Rita Hayworth.

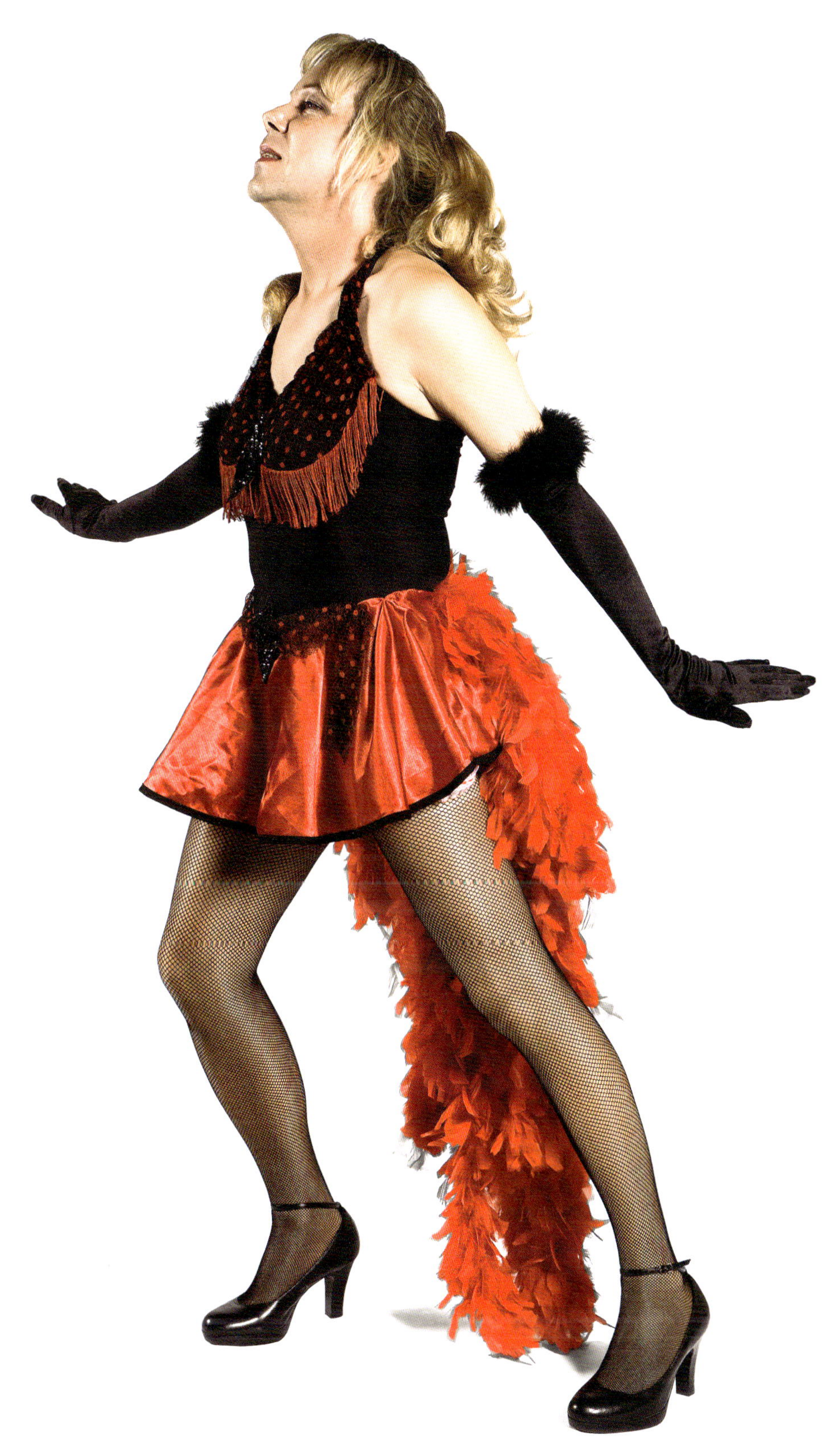

DAVID — RABBI

At synagogue I normally wear a suit and tie, but I try to remember that somehow underneath I am wearing leather.

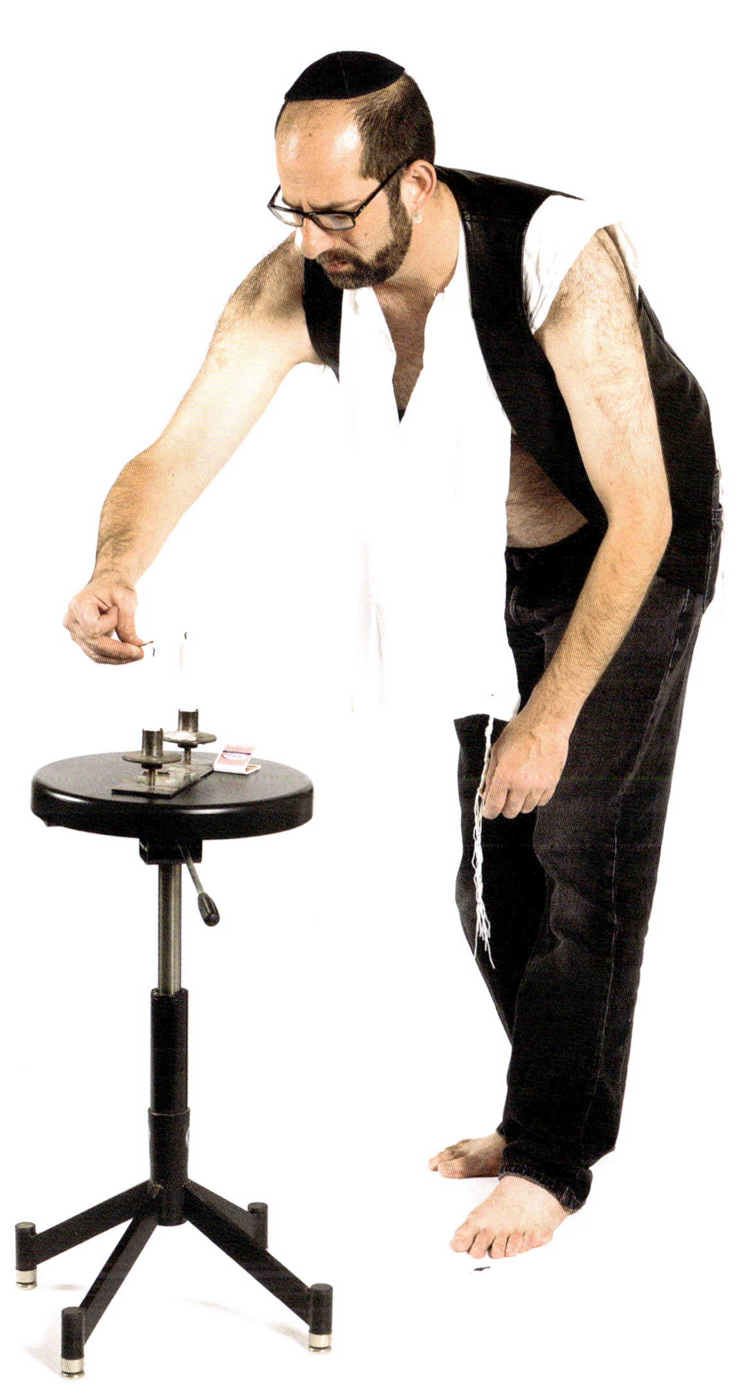

PAUL — WRITER

My inner self is a classical violinist, though I am not classical, and I don't play an instrument.

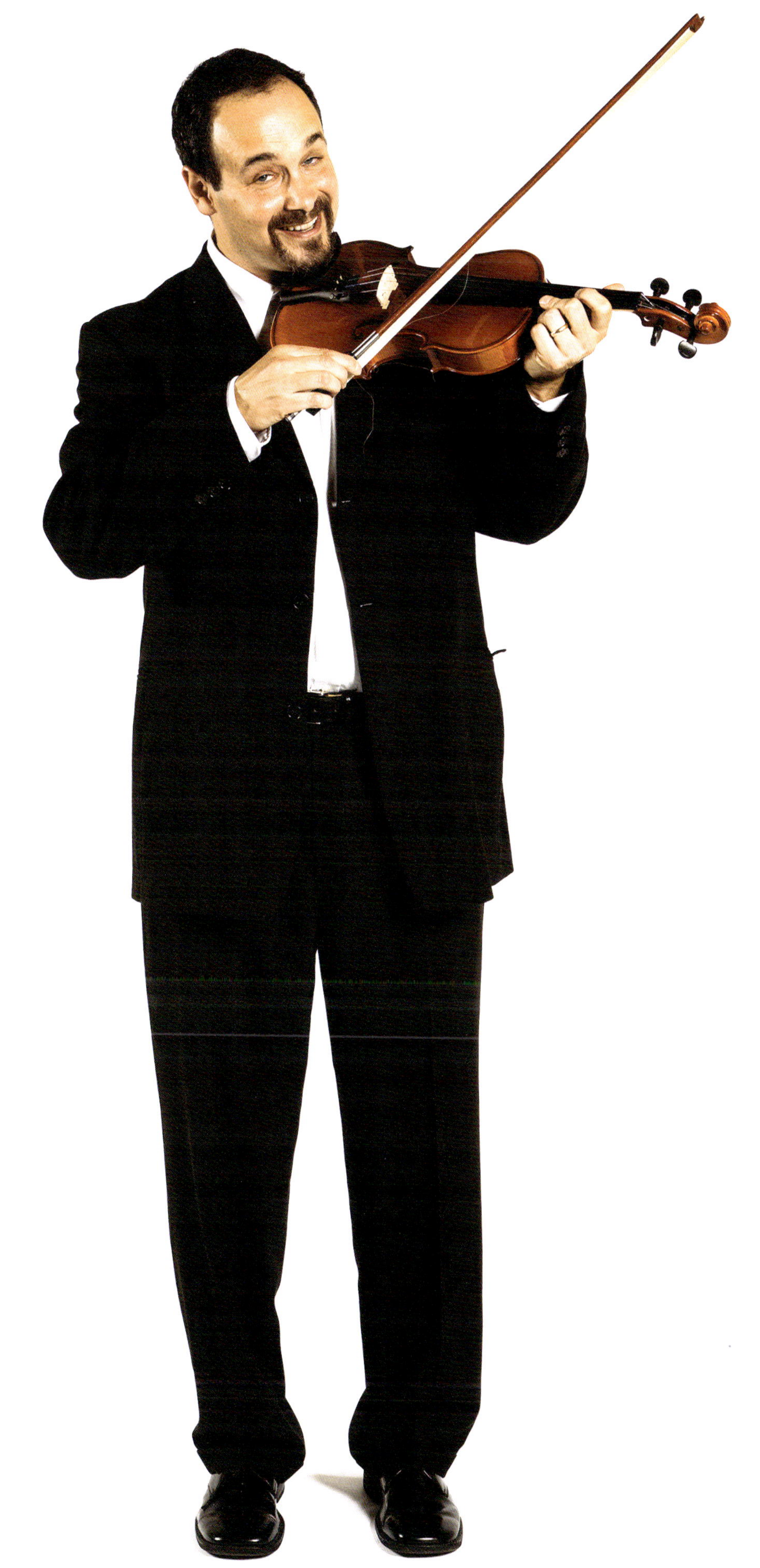

DAWN — FORMER JUNIOR LEAGUE PRESIDENT

I was physically, emotionally, and psychologically abused… I was outed by my husband… I am a fighter—stripped bare, but I keep on swinging.

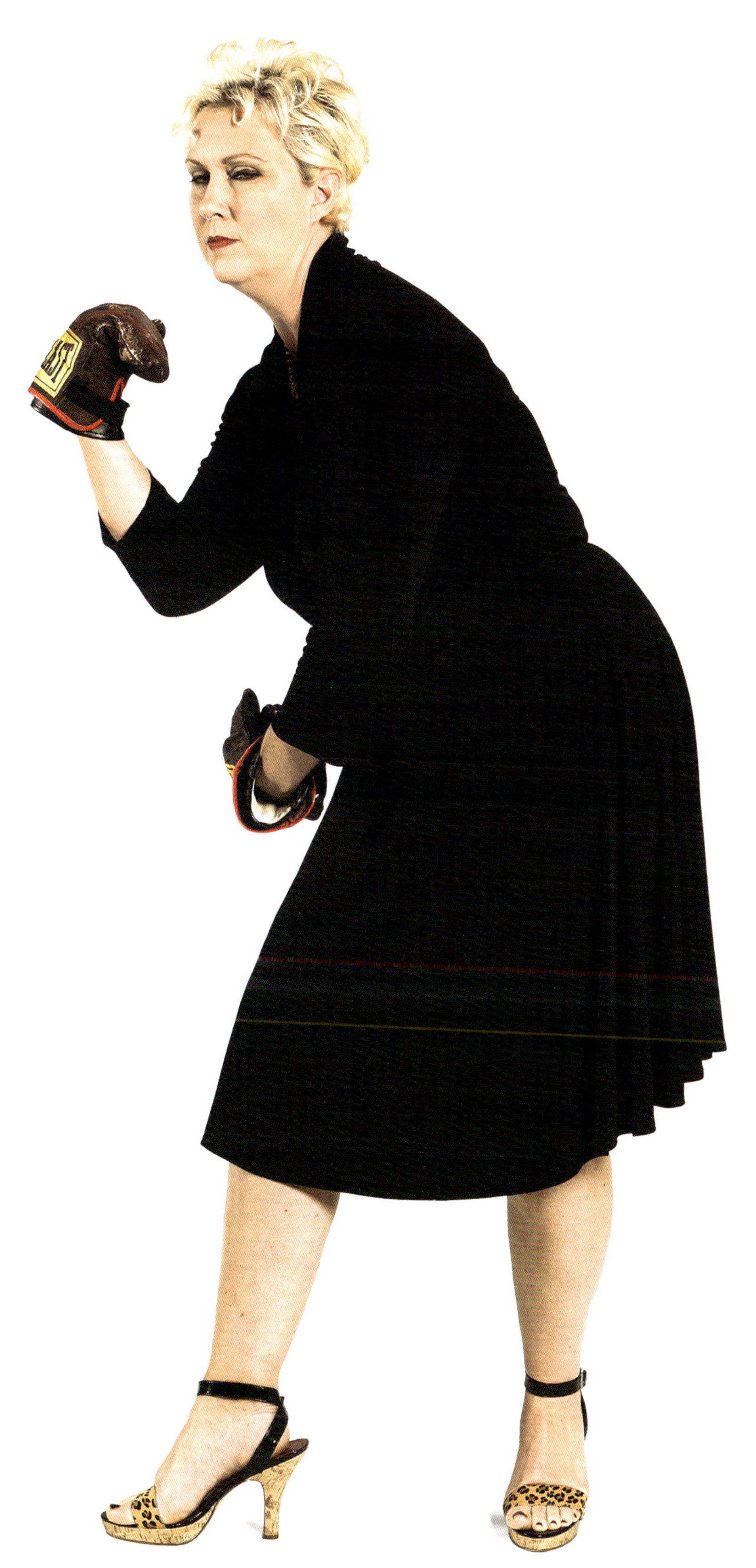

AIMEE — TATTOO AND BODY PIERCING

I like being a girl… no one knows I am a woman, let alone a lesbian. My beard is natural, there is no imbalance.

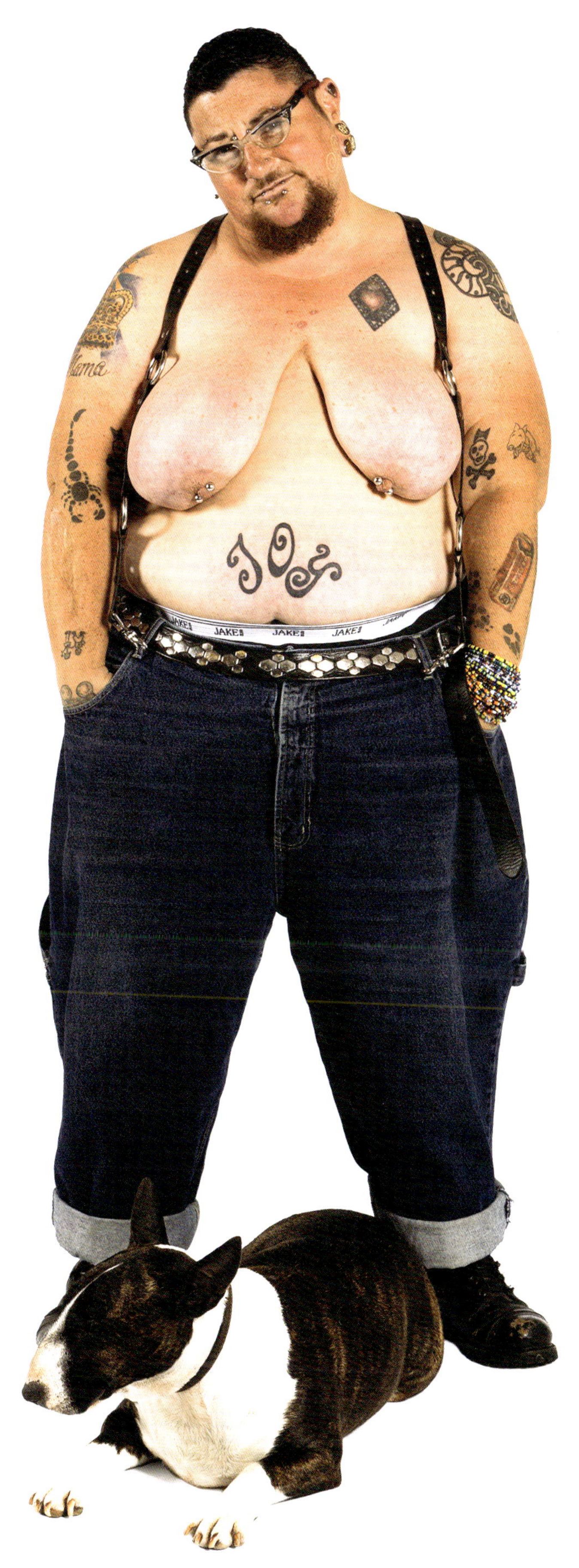
JAKE

BARRY — BOOK DESIGNER, ILLUSTRATOR

I am my dog… I don't want to get into the corny stuff about fidelity… for me it goes a little bit deeper.

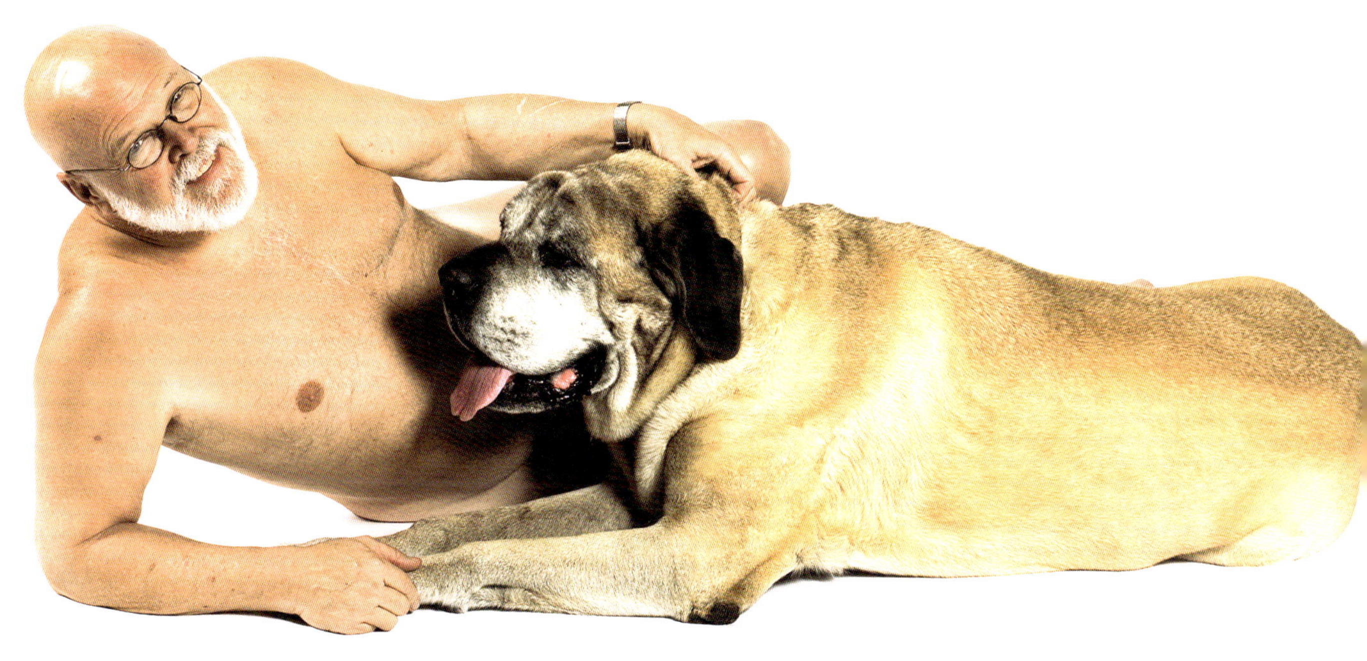

ROBIN — GRAPHIC DESIGNER

I am a being made completely of light, trapped in a bag full of bones.

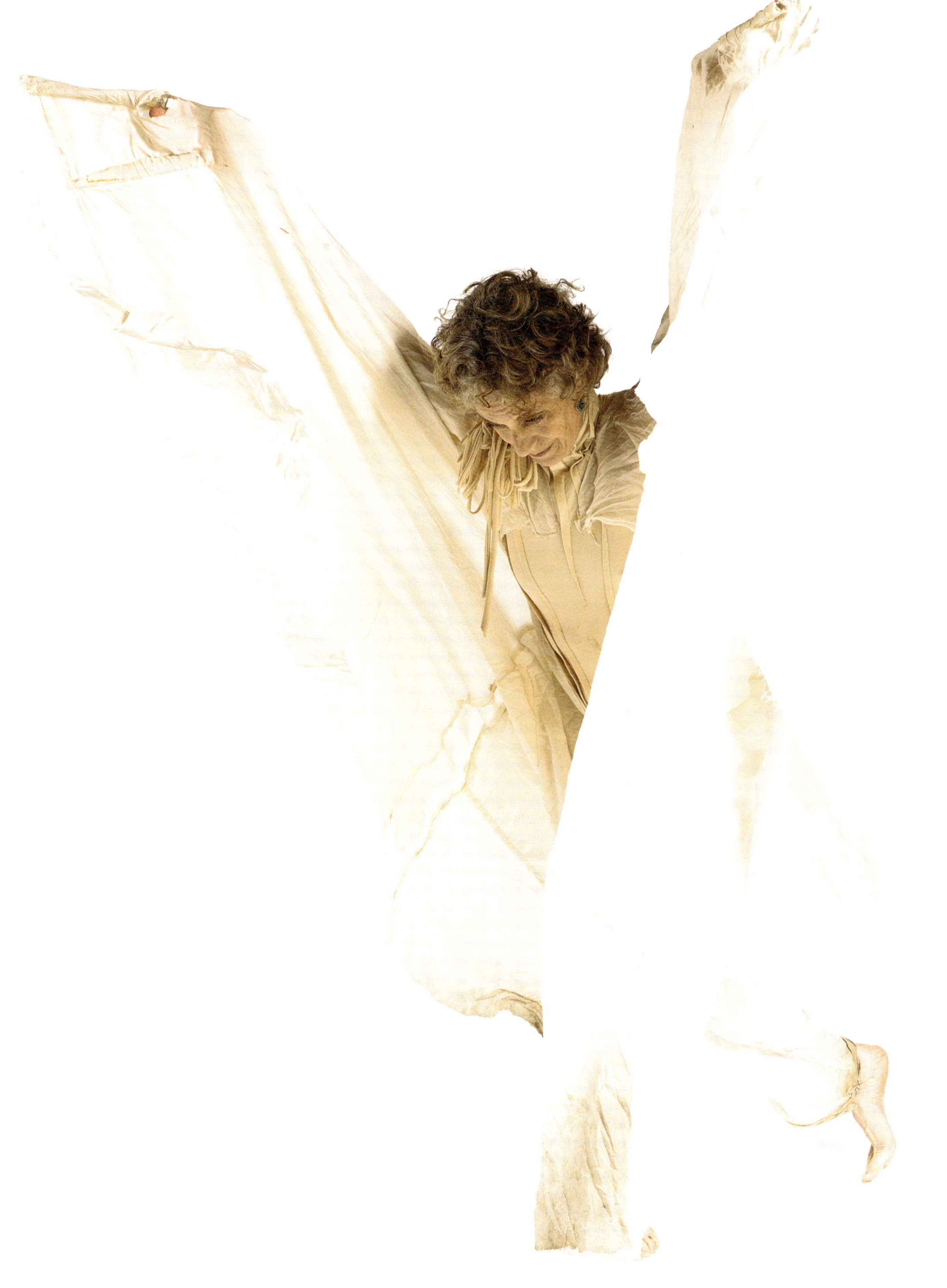

CHRISTOPHER — EPISCOPAL PRIEST

The truth is there is a dark side of me. It's often difficult to express that in my occupation.

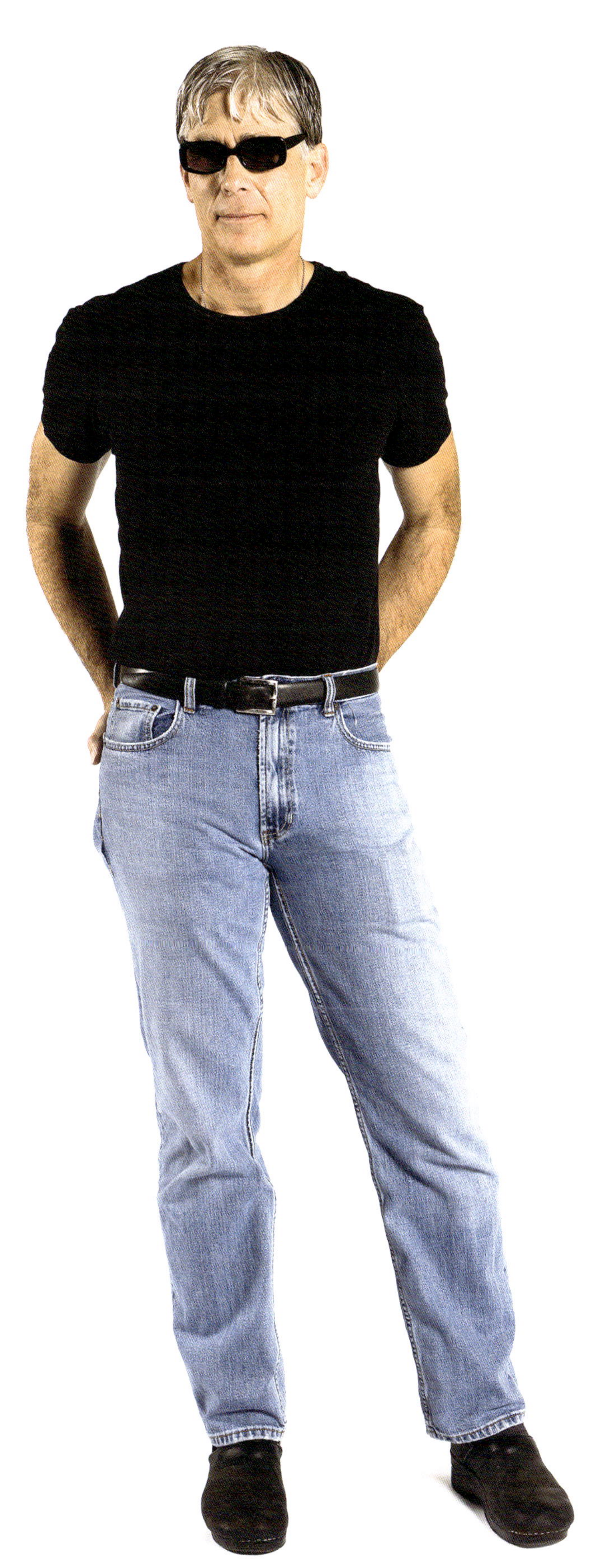

KRIS — ARTIST

The outfit is a cross between masculinity and femininity…
I just have two different sides that come out depending on the day.

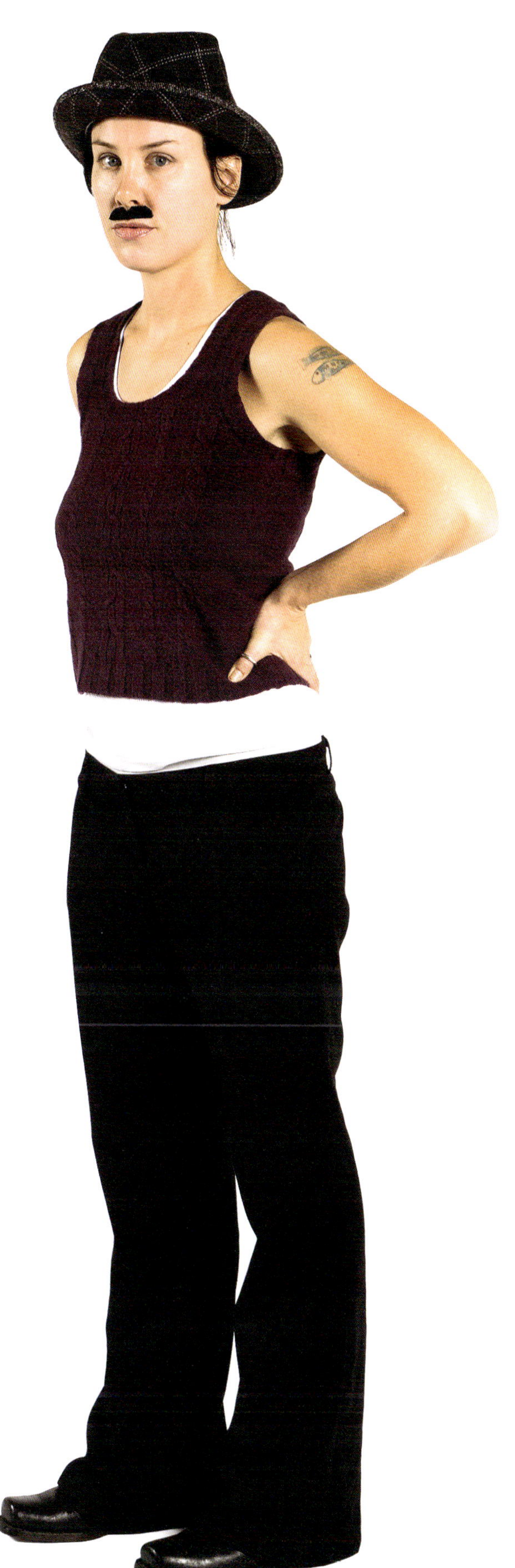

IRA — ADVERTISING FIRM CEO

My secret self is a wizard who takes illusions and makes people think they are real.

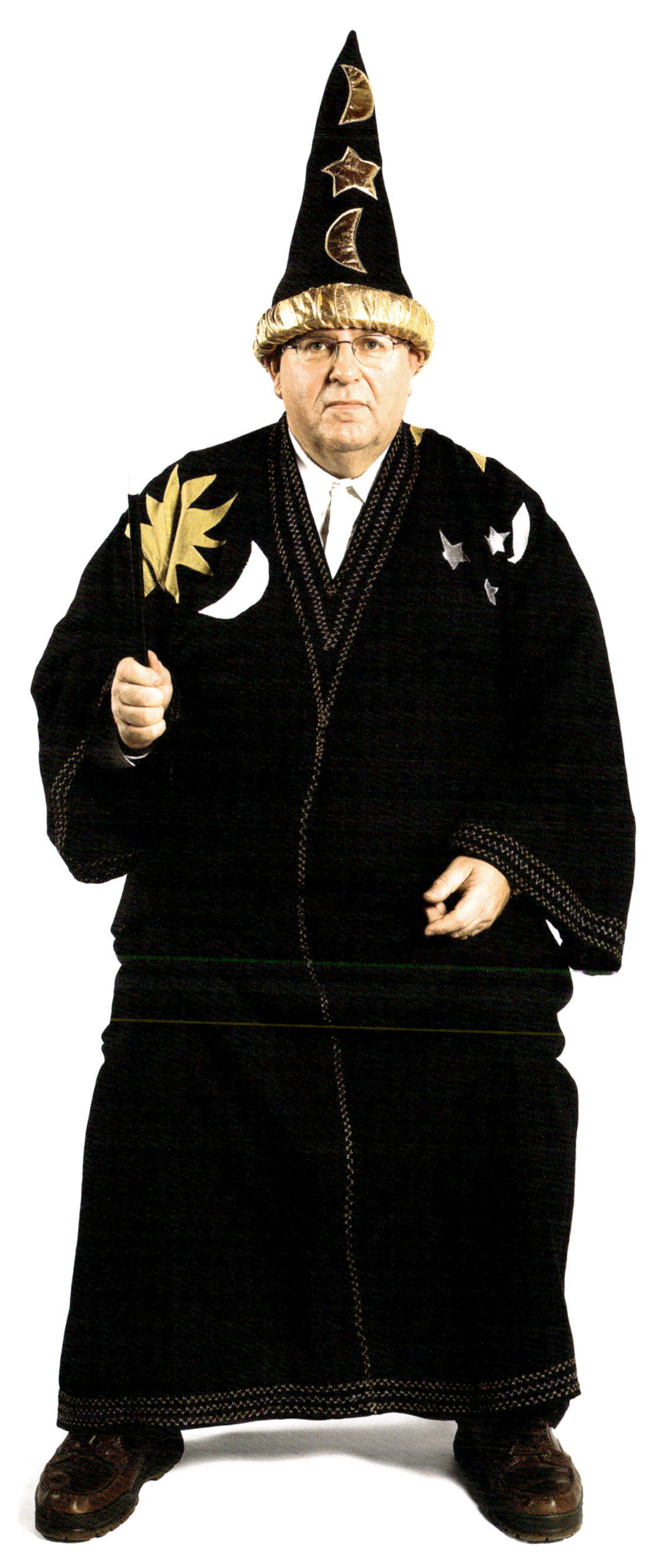

MARTÍN AND KLEMENTE — POET/STUDENT

Since I grew up in east New York I always wanted to be a gangster.
Chad the Great White Shark hunts lawyers, the most dangerous game.

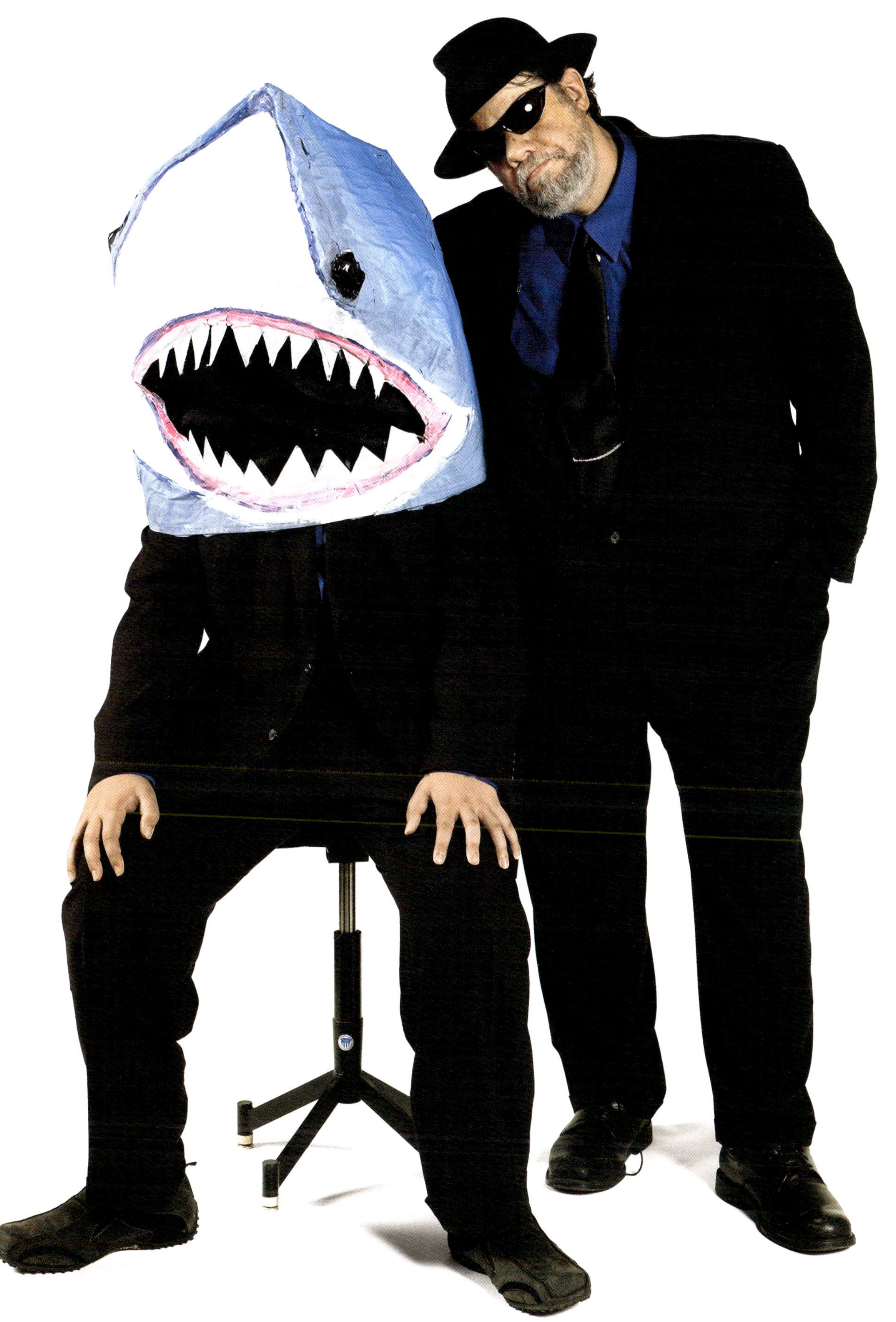

KARLA — ARTIST

I am a painter of happy, colorful Judaica.
My secret self is provocative...

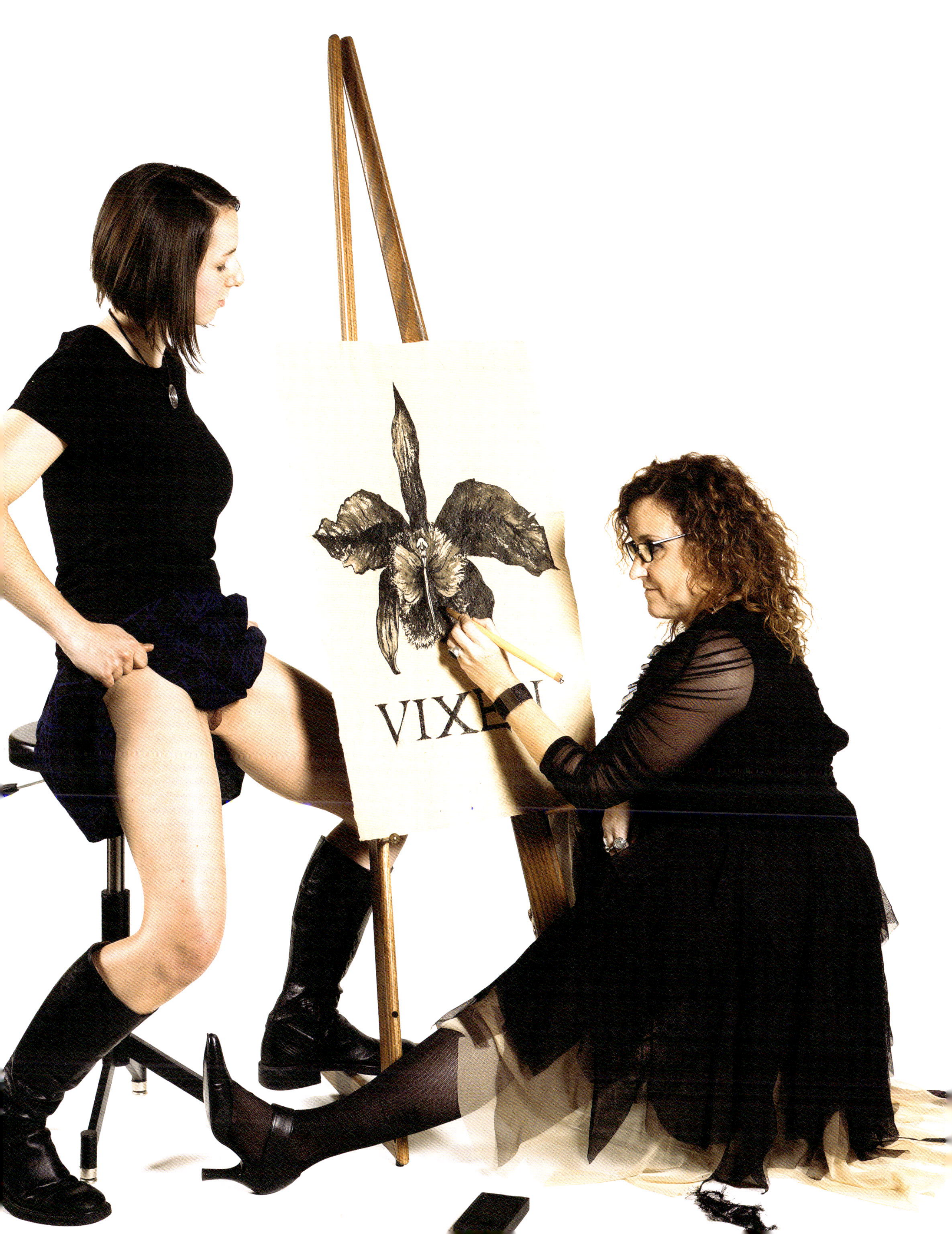
VIXE

PAUL — GALLERY DIRECTOR

*The Buddha says just let it go... so far I still have that drive.
I am looking for a way to reconcile it.*

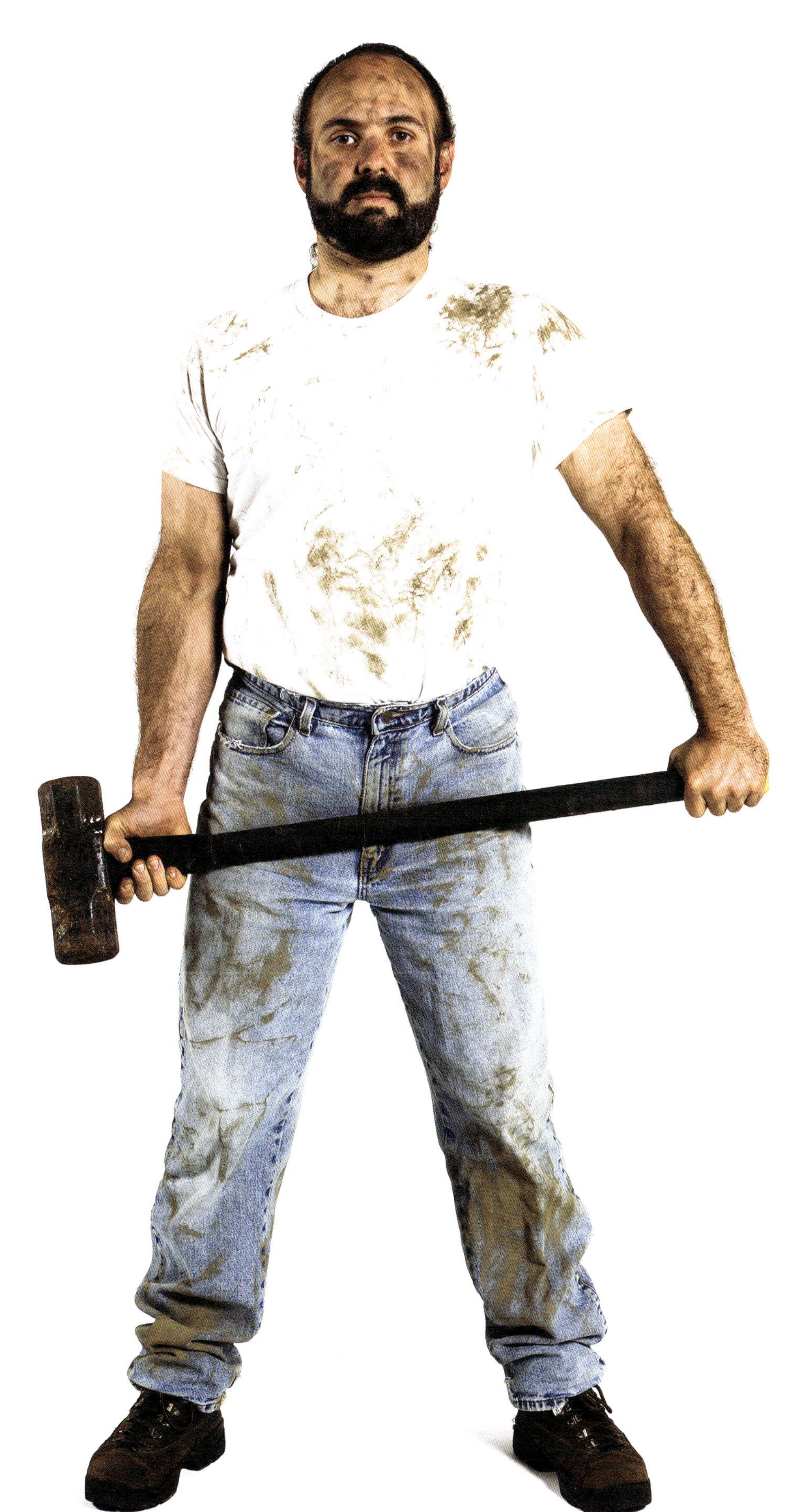

POSTURES OF THE DREAM: LEONARD NIMOY'S *SECRET SELVES*

BY JOHN STOMBERG

We see only postures of the dream,
Riders of the motion that swings the face
Into view under evening skies, with no
False disarray as proof of authenticity.

— from John Ashbery, "Self Portrait in a Convex Mirror"

Every posed portrait is an act of negotiation between subject and image-maker. Given time to prepare the sitter contributes to the construction of the self captured by the portraitist. Describing just this phenomenon in photography, the German philosopher and historian Golo Mann proposes that: "When someone is trying to be natural, or better, when he does not know he is being photographed, he reveals character. But if he approaches the camera with a certain solemnity, with the intent of showing himself off, he has become something more than himself: he is revealing a secret self-image."[1] For his recent photographic portrait series, *Secret Selves*, Leonard Nimoy fosters this exact scenario, creating conditions conducive to self-revelation, and capitalizing on the special relationship that develops between a willing sitter and a sensitive photographer.

Producing *Secret Selves* entailed complications on both sides of the camera that shaped the project as a whole. First, Nimoy asked his sitters to be prepared to reveal their secret selves. They arrived ready to re-present themselves in a guise they felt was unknown or at least not immediately apparent. Their participation in the sittings triggered a convoluted role-playing. In order to achieve their goal of self-revelation they must display their secret self and repress their usual, visible

1. Golo Mann, "Forward," in *August Sander: Men without Masks* (Greenwich, CT: New York Graphic Society, 1971), p.7.

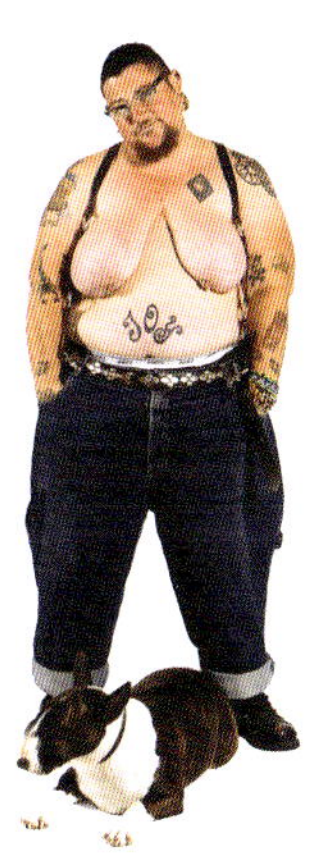

FIG. 1.
Aimee — Tattoo and Body Piercing, 2007.
Archival pigment print

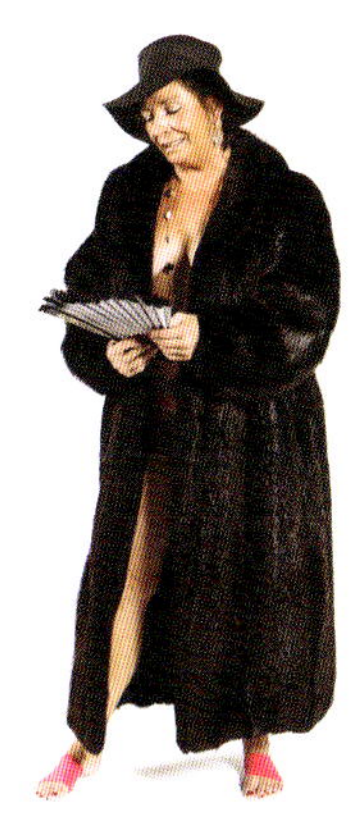

FIG. 2.
Natalie — Foster Care Mother, 2007.
Archival pigment print

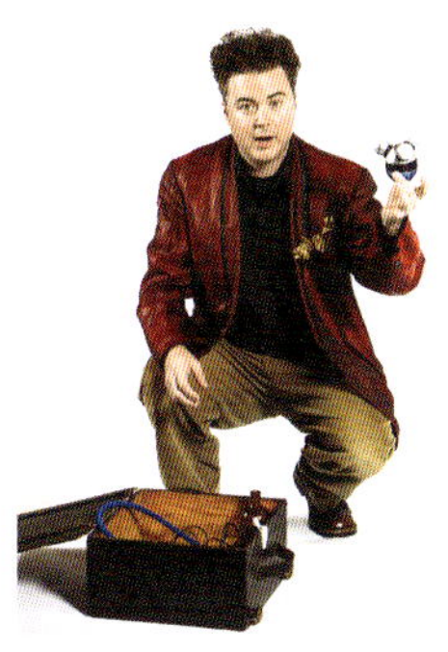

FIG. 3.
James — Newspaper Arts Editor, 2007.
Archival pigment print

persona. For Carl Jung, this process formed the core of meaningful psychoanalysis. In a critical early essay he writes: "The persona is a complicated system of relations between individual consciousness and society, fittingly enough a kind of mask, designed on the one hand to make a definite impression upon others, and, on the other, to conceal the true nature of the individual."[2] Nimoy's deceptively simple request inspires his sitters to consider and make manifest one of the most essential and complex psychological dilemmas that humans face: who are we, really?

Then there are the deeper layers of complication that Nimoy's own fame brings to the pictures. To find his subjects, Nimoy's gallerist in Northampton, Massachusetts, sent letters inviting the recipients to "show your secret self to Leonard Nimoy." Both parts of the invitation are key: "show your secret self" and "to Leonard Nimoy." As a photographer, Nimoy had to somehow acknowledge his celebrity and the fact that it would matter in the already complex relationship he would have with his sitters. It seems likely that people would show up with some side of themselves that they wished to share with Leonard Nimoy specifically. This might well be a different face than they would present to either an unknown photographer or one for whom the topic of identity was less germane.

Nimoy's concept for his *Secret Selves* project, as he explains it, comes from something that Aristophanes said at Plato's *Symposium* circa 385 B.C.E. Aristophanes speculated that all human beings were but half of their original self. In his view, there were originally three sexes: men, women, and the combination of both. Each person was defined by four legs, four arms, and two faces looking in opposite directions. Over time these ancient beings became insolent to the gods, who in response sent Zeus to earth to weaken their spirits. This he did by dividing them in two, cleaving all humans down the middle, leaving a blank area (our backs) where once we were conjoined to our other half. Typically, according to Aristophanes, men split from a dual male pair continued to seek out the company of other men, hoping to

2. C.G. Jung, "The Relations between the Ego and the Unconscious" (1928), in *The Collected Works of C. G. Jung, Volume 7: Two Essays on Analytical Psychology*, ed. and trans. by Gerhard Adler and R.F.C. Hull (Princeton, NJ: Princeton University Press, 1967), p. 305.

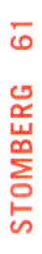

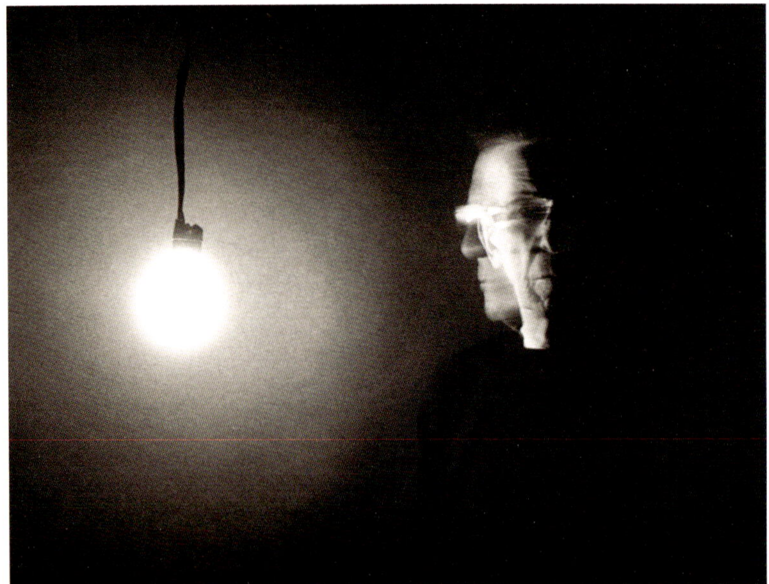

FIG. 4.
Leonard Nimoy, *Double Self Portrait with Lightbulb*, 2003. Gelatin silver print. Courtesy the artist and R. Michelson Galleries

complete their split selves; likewise with split women pairs. The androgynous pairs continued to search out members of the opposite sex and became the breeders of the race. Regardless of the original gender of the pair, all humans now pined for their missing halves.

Resuscitating Aristophanes' idea as a metaphor, Nimoy postulates that we all have a secret side that combines with our more overt selves to form a complete being. For his *Secret Selves* project he encourages sitters to help him unmask the unseen aspects of their whole self. They arrive having decided to reveal something they know about themselves but do not typically share. For many this leads to posing either nude or partially nude. In the case of *Aimee — Tattoo and Body Piercing*, she has removed just her shirt... but that is just enough [FIG. 1]. We are forced to reconcile the incongruity of beard and breasts — simultaneous markers of opposite gender identity. In addition to this confusion of typical gender indicators, the portrait contains many clues about the individual who is our subject. Several piercings and tattoos — including the word "JOY" across her abdomen — identify this sitter as someone in particular, and with disarming intimacy. She has seen to it that the rich tapestry of her personality cannot be reduced to stereotype. It is pointless to quibble about which self is the real one — the one lived daily or the person she reveals to the photographer on this occasion. Nimoy works, as do his sitters, to allow a multifaceted personality to emerge, trusting in the camera's ability to arrest the variables into one coherent image.

The sitters reveal their alternate identity in a manner that, by the nature of the setting — lights, a backdrop, an audience — has many of the characteristics of a performance. Once the session begins, Nimoy directs, waiting for the sitter's ideas and his to come together with a synchronicity that seems true to him. In a short, telling film documenting his work and accompanying this exhibition, we hear Nimoy speaking with his subjects, putting them at ease, making suggestions, and finally exclaiming, "Got it!" *Natalie — Foster Care Mother*, for example, has been celibate for years and has decided to pose nude mostly as a way to trigger a return to a sexually active lifestyle [FIG. 2]. For her, the photograph will be secondary to the therapeutic experience of being nude in the presence of a man. She cries as she explains this to Nimoy, who reassures her, earning her trust as they begin working on her portrait. She has selected limited props to help reveal her dormant sexuality: fur coat, floppy hat, earrings and necklace, light pink foot wraps, and a fan at which she stares wistfully. In the implicit contract between the two, she acts out her missing half (her neglected sexual side), and Nimoy works to capture that elusive identity photographically.

These manifest identities also can be red herrings, diversionary truths covering still deeper and more complex realities. Nimoy asked the sitters in advance for a brief written statement describing their ordinary and secret selves. Upon meeting them, and with this statement in hand, he draws them into discussion. This conversation lies at the heart of the process. One young man, *James — Newspaper Arts Editor*, for example, wrote of his desire to be a research scientist who invents wondrous objects [FIG. 3]. As Nimoy talks with him though, a more humorous, trickster personality emerges, one who takes youthful delight in the silly ideas of the objects he has ostensibly invented. Nimoy depicts the man squatting next to his suitcase full of pseudo-inventions. Taking up a fraction of the space framed by the photograph, Nimoy makes the inventor appear diminutive, reinforcing his childlike presence. In this instance, Nimoy works to get beyond the surface of the persona that the sitter presented; rather than documenting the proffered identity, Nimoy's image cuts deeper.

Concerns about identity pervade much of Nimoy's recent photographic work. Despite a career marked with landmark stage and film performances, for many people Nimoy's identity is subsumed in that of Mr. Spock, the character he played in the Star Trek television series.[3] For Nimoy, the phenomenal success of this character has led him to a fascinating series of personal investigations into the competing forces of self and persona. He reveals some of his thoughts on these issues in two autobiographies, *I Am Not Spock* (1975) and *I Am Spock* (1995).[4] In the first he discusses the period of his life shortly after the original series came to an end:

> There were a lot of emotional crosscurrents operating for me at this time. Obviously, the work being offered was coming as a direct result of my impact as Mr. Spock. On the other hand, I was involved in something of a crusade to develop a reputation as an actor with some range... At this point I went through a definite identity crisis. The question was whether to embrace Mr. Spock or to fight the onslaught of public interest. I realize now that I really had no choice in the matter. Spock and Star Trek were very much alive and there wasn't anything that I could do to change that.[5]

When Nimoy returned to the subject 20 years later, his views had developed a new analytical sharpness. Of course, he is Mr. Spock — he created the character and spent a meaningful part of his professional acting life furthering it. In this formulation — which seems distinctly relevant for the *Secret Selves* series — Nimoy posits his persona as a sort of secret self, always seeking the modes and means of its own representation.

Since returning to his passion for photography, Nimoy has created several powerful self-portraits that give visual form to the ideas of duality and ancillary identity that he took up in his autobiographies. In one photograph he depicts himself in three-quarter length, looking both forward and sideways simultaneously, suggesting two individuals in one [FIG. 4]. There is an indistinct passage in the image where his head is moving too fast to be captured in focus, blurring the distinction between the two faces, and reinforcing the notion that the fine line between one's various selves is impossible to find.

In his professional life, Nimoy lives in a world of self-revelation and role-playing. (In addition to his career in Hollywood, imagine years of attending Star Trek conventions and meeting hundreds of thousands of ardent fans, many of whom probably seem all too eager to shed their day-to-day identities in favor of one associated with the series.) Anyone familiar with Nimoy's life and career, anyone responding positively to the invitation that was the genesis of the *Secret Selves* series, must have given more than a passing thought to notions of self and persona, life and acting, and the ways in which each is manifested through visual language. Nimoy's identity thus becomes a significant factor in the images.

3. The original series, in which the Spock character was launched, ran on television for only three seasons, from 1966 to 1969; the films began to appear in 1979, with the latest debuting in 2009.

4. Leonard Nimoy, *I Am Not Spock* (Millbrae, California: Celestial Arts, 1975) and Leonard Nimoy, *I Am Spock* (New York: Hyperion Books, 1995).

5. Nimoy, *I Am Not Spock*, p. 62.

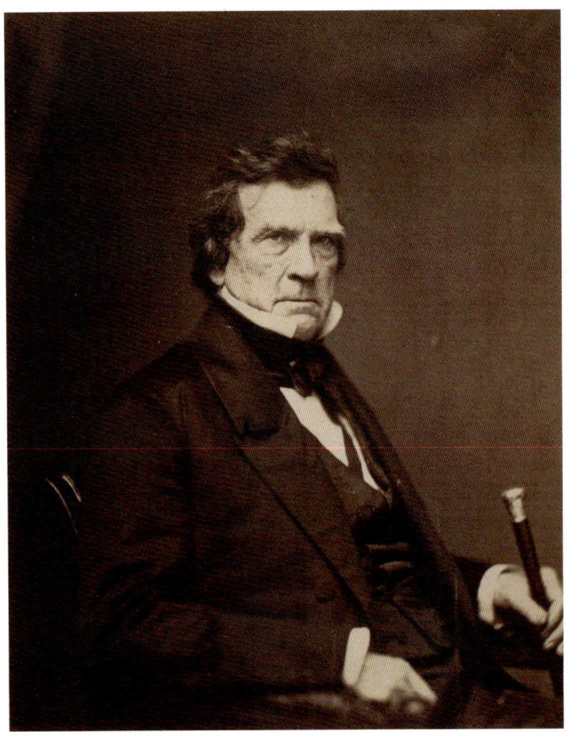

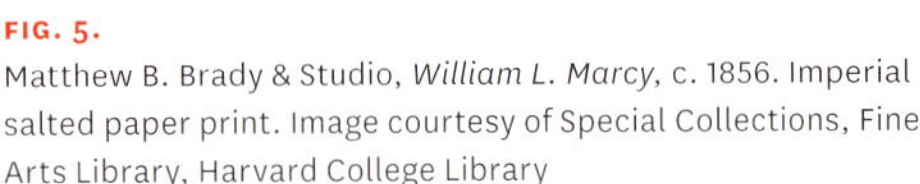

FIG. 5.
Matthew B. Brady & Studio, *William L. Marcy*, c. 1856. Imperial salted paper print. Image courtesy of Special Collections, Fine Arts Library, Harvard College Library

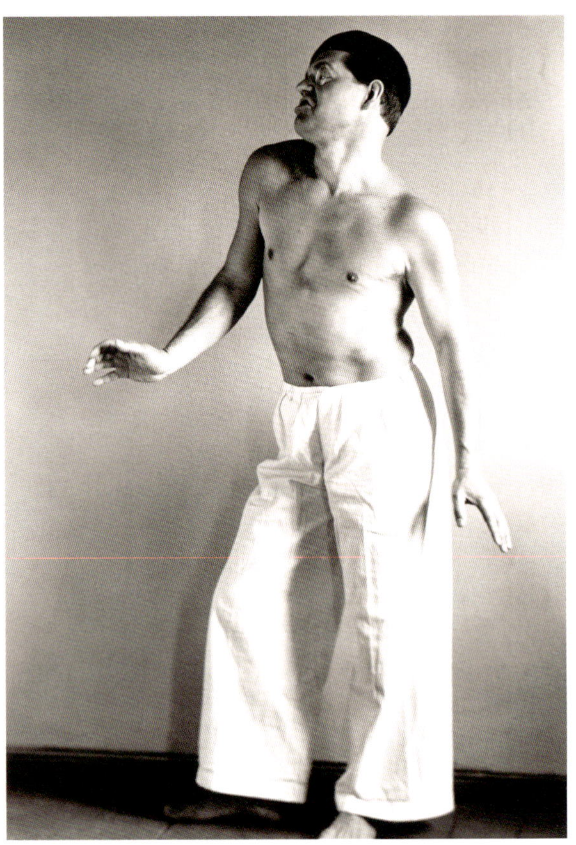

FIG. 6.
August Sander, *Raoul Hausmann as Dancer*, 1929. Gelatin silver print. © Die Photographische Sammlung/SK Stiftung Kultur — August Sander Archiv, Cologne; ARS, New York, 2010

If it is important in understanding these works to account for the special internal dynamics set in motion from Nimoy's celebrity status, then it is just as important to understand the work's position within the broader context of the history of portrait photography. For his *Secret Selves* project Nimoy set up in Northampton a temporary portrait studio, a place for the creation of new work and not, significantly, for the discovery of pre-existing images. His approach (essentially akin to the agrarian impulse) can be understood in opposition to that of hunter/gatherer photographers who wander the world looking for images to capture and frame. He constructs an environment in which he creates rather than discovers images.

Nimoy's photographic practice relates directly to that of his photography professor, Robert Heinecken, an artist who also focused on a studio approach. Heinecken founded the photography department at UCLA in the 1960s, and by the early 1970s, when Nimoy worked with him, he had a reputation for using the medium irreverently, adding collage, magazine images, drawing, and painting. Essential to Heinecken's practice was the idea of always creating something entirely new and not simply reflecting exterior realities. He had little interest in the ideology surrounding documentary photography, for example, and famously argued that "many pictures turn out to be limp translations of the known world instead of vital objects which create an intrinsic world of their own.

There is a vast difference between taking a picture and making a photograph."[6] Nimoy clearly "makes" photographs in the Heinecken sense.

In Nimoy's temporary studio, variables are limited or tightly regulated; much of the expressive force has to be achieved by the sitters themselves. His studio becomes, as Alan Trachtenberg writes about Mathew Brady's, a "theater of desire."[7] Visitors to Nimoy's studio, like those to Brady's more than a century prior, appear with expectations of specific revelations in the photographs. For Brady's sitters — partially by virtue of the fame of the studio itself — the goal was social and political advancement [FIG. 5]. His studio was the center of his *The Gallery of Illustrious Americans* project, so the fact of being photographed by Brady held in it the promise of social advance and possibly even lasting fame. Nimoy's sitters bring a different sort of "desire" to his studio, one far more personal. Brady's sitters sought an image that would identify them with factors external to the self — that is, to be seen. Nimoy's subjects come in search of internal revelations — that is, to see.

Brady's forte was the three-quarter, bust-length view; Nimoy favors a full-standing figure against a neutral background. This rather shallow depth of field and the constrained lateral dimensions of this staging limit the input that a sitter's surroundings can add to a portrait, and at the same time forces the viewer to focus on the individual portrayed. We find a similar compositional strategy in much of August Sander's portrait work of the 1920s. Sander, for example, posed Raoul Hausmann, an artist and dada provocateur, in an amorphous interior quite similar to that used by Nimoy [FIG. 6]. Hausmann's personality stands out vividly against the neutral backdrop. Sander, who began his career as a commercial portraitist, used this approach sparingly. More typically he posed subjects in settings that amplified their exterior trappings — a secretary at a desk, a baker in the kitchen and so forth — which had to do with the overarching goal for his work, namely to seek out types of people in society and not individuals. On the other hand, many of his most telling portraits of individuals, such as Hausmann's, utilize the more generic backdrop.

There is something both challenging and liberating in setting severe limitations on the variables in a creative endeavor. Nimoy, like Sander and others before him, capitalizes on the uncanny possibilities offered by the juxtaposition of figures floated against a neutral background. Other artists in other media have given themselves similar limitations as a way of focusing on depth rather than breadth. This has been especially true for 20th-century artists such as Joseph Albers who spent decades painting squares, or Sol LeWitt who for years limited himself to primary colors and lines moving in four directions. This aesthetic discipline led to great discoveries for both artists as they realized the potential of strict confines. The photographic portrait equivalent of these practices has been explored to great advantage by numerous photographers, but perhaps none with as much interest as two thoroughly distinct American portraitists — Mike Disfarmer and Irving Penn.

Mike Disfarmer ran a small portrait studio in Heber Springs, Arkansas, between 1939 and 1945 [FIG. 7].[8] His deceptively simple compositions (most often shot against neutral backdrops) belie the care with which he lit and positioned his sitters. One imagines that the elaborate preparation process — Disfarmer was known to take up to an hour to set up each shot — allowed him to recognize the story each portrait should tell. Getting to know the sitters as they arranged themselves (many of whom arrived quasi-costumed, or at least in their Sunday best) gave him time to watch them interact with each other and with him. The emotional and expressive range of Heber citizens was no less varied than those of Northampton, if the clothing and props were far more vernacular in Disfarmer's studio. Though we do not know the individual sitters, we identify with them because their body language, gestures, and facial expressions transmit basic, recognizable human emotions: we can feel their

6. Quoted in Michael Ned Holty, "Robert Heinecken: Mark Selwyn Fine Art," *Artforum* vol. 47, issue 6 (February 2009): p. 199.

7. The *entire* sentence reads: "Not a museum of natural history, however, but a theater of desire, the gallery had become a new kind of city place devoted to performance: The making of oneself over into a social image." Alan Trachtenberg, *Reading American Photographs: Images as History, Mathew Brady to Walker Evans* (New York: Hill and Wang, 1990), 40.

8. For further reading on Disfarmer, see Toba Tucker, *Heber Springs Portraits: Continuity and Change in the World Disfarmer Photographed* (Albuquerque, NM: University of New Mexico Press, 1996).

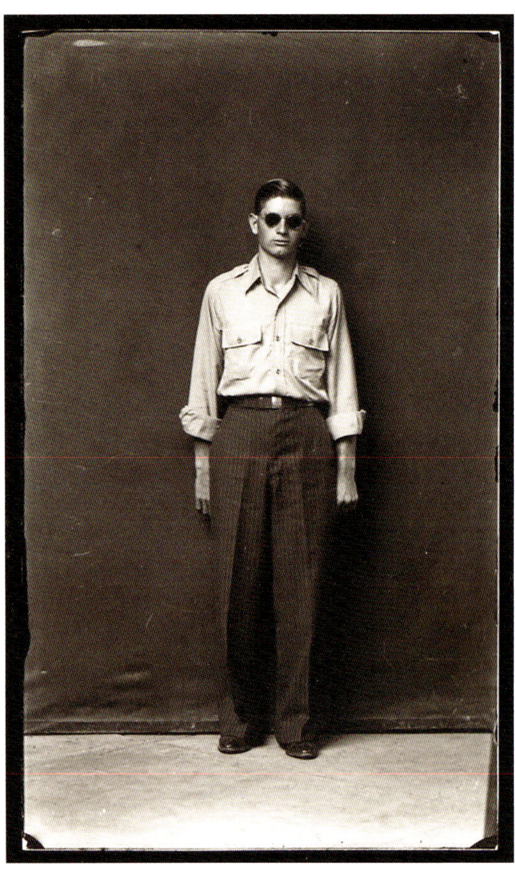

FIG. 7.
Mike Disfarmer, *Young Man in Sunglasses*, ca. 1942–45. Silver halide print on paper made from original glass negative © Peter Miller

secret hopes, worries, and aspirations, and we feel we know something about small-town life in mid-20th century America because of it. We can also feel Disfarmer's sometimes cranky manner reflected back through the sometimes uncomfortable, discomforting poses, especially the images of children. Whereas Nimoy puts his subjects at ease, Disfarmer more often than not seemed to set them on edge.

Irving Penn's career was a world away from Disfarmer's, but he too made much of his best work with individuals placed before a plain grey paper backdrop. Penn, a renowned fashion photographer working primarily for *Vogue* after World War II, approached his portrait work with a distinct passion and aesthetic sensibility unusual for commissioned work. Like Nimoy, Penn created an open, revelatory atmosphere. Writing about a session with Penn, for example, the anthropologist Lionel Tiger wrote: "The act became a duet... I was a performer not even of my own self, but in the context of something new to me, which demanded a highly complex effort. I had both some grasp of distance from myself, and yet a full sense of immersion in that person who was Penn's subject.... I recall the sense of giving more than I had, of being more than I was, of telling more than my story... a symmetry of intent between myself and Penn seemed to have become created."[9]

Nimoy establishes a similar "symmetry of intent" for his *Secret Selves* sessions. This is evident especially in the images of people whose revelations lean towards fantasy and whimsy. In *Tammy — Ex Marine/Teacher for*

9. Lionel Tiger, "Encounter," *Camera Arts* (September–October, 1981), pp. 43–44, quoted in John Szarkowski, *Irving Penn* (New York: Museum of Modern Art, 1984): 27.

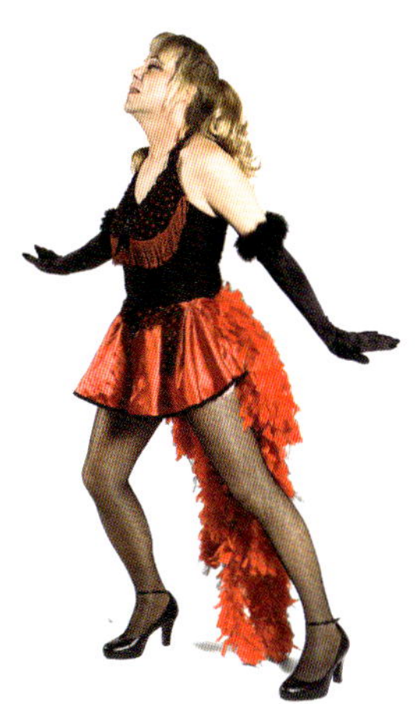

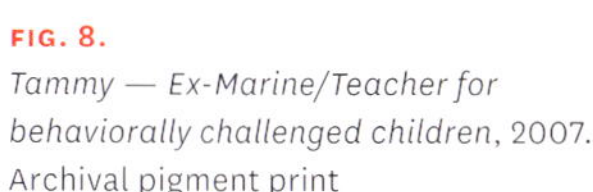

FIG. 8.
Tammy — Ex-Marine/Teacher for behaviorally challenged children, 2007.
Archival pigment print

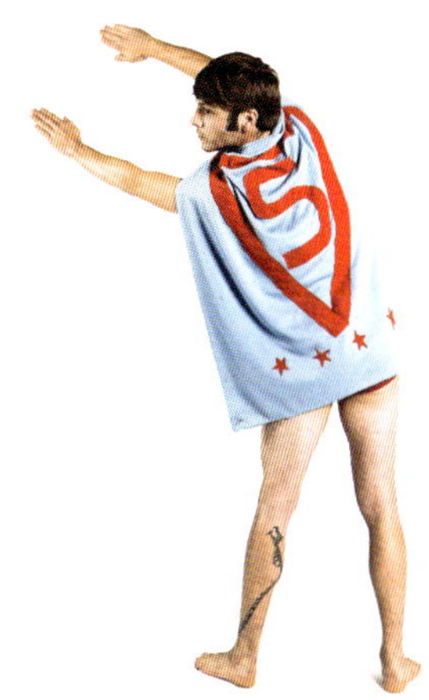

FIG. 9.
Joseph — U.S. Navy, 2007.
Archival pigment print

behaviorally challenged children and *Joseph — U.S. Navy* Nimoy has created a safe zone in which these individuals demonstrate a yearning that takes them far away from their current existence **[FIGS. 8 & 9]**. The dancer strikes a pose at once of dance and of flight. Eyes closed, arms thrown back, she appears to relish the wind rushing across her airborne body. The caped man is prepared for flight. He raises his arms and looks back to the photographer as though for reassurance that he has the correct flying posture. Both perform sincerely, working with Nimoy to articulate and share a desired existence.

The last decade has seen many large-scale photographic projects of sweeping scope and ambition: most seek — covertly or overtly — to discover, name, and characterize a specific category of people within society. They search for cultural rather individual identity. These projects define characteristics that visually join individuals into sociological groups. Rather than the duet that Tiger describes, we feel the presence of the photographer's organizing choreography in projects such as Tina Barney's *The Europeans*, Peter Hugo's *The Hyena Men*, Daniela Rossell's *Ricas y Famosas: Mexico, 1994–2001*, Katy Grannan's *The Westerns*, or Liu Zheng's *The Chinese* (among many others). While Nimoy's selection of people certainly qualifies as a subset of society, such a broad, sociological characterization is clearly not the goal of the project. We never feel in these works that Nimoy is trying to capture the essential Northampton. Instead he assists individuals in making their own self-portraits. Like a film director he works to draw the most out of his actors. But unlike a narrative film, he has not assigned the roles they play. His interest lies in their personal stories, aspirations, and yearning.

When John Ashbery wrote the lines that appear at the beginning of this essay, he was transfixed by a famous Italian Mannerist self-portrait.[10] His poem revels in the potential for portraits to both reveal and shape identity. For the *Secret Selves* project, Nimoy works to bring together the ingredients necessary to capture the posture of his sitters' dreams in his studio. It is a simple studio, a light-infused place that is no place; and this is perhaps the ultimate secret to the project's interest and success: Nimoy's willingness to work towards portraits "with no/False disarray as proof of authenticity."

10. Parmigianino's *Self-Portrait in a Convex Mirror* of 1524 in the Kunsthistorisches Museum, Vienna.

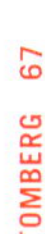

BEHIND THE SCENES

Let me begin by acknowledging the elephant in the room. Many of you picked up this book because of the name on the cover. Some of you might not generally peruse photography or fine art books. Some of you are predisposed to like what you see, while others might expect only the work of a "dabbler" or "celebrity photographer." I see this every day in my gallery. People stop in out of curiosity, often skeptical and ready to dismiss; but they leave as converts, appreciative of a refined artistic skill and vision. (Leonard Nimoy has been engaged with photography since he was 13 years old, a serious student and practitioner of the art form.) When I first exhibited Leonard's photographs, I called up some of the best collectors I know and invited them to see a "new artist I was considering taking on." In thirty years I'd never heard such enthusiasm. Only when they had confirmed my own judgement of the work did I mention the name of this new artist. The work speaks for itself.

Crowds flock to museums to see a Picasso, or a LeWitt, and they are naturally curious about the life of the creator. But the art that keeps us coming back tells us less about the artist than it does about ourselves, or about our "secret selves." This brings me to the "production" of the *Secret Selves* studio shoot. "Who are these people," I am asked continually, even though the sitters are showing you who they are in this book. What I am really being asked is "Where did you find the subjects, and why didn't you call me?"

So here is a peek at the process behind the scenes:

It began with an email I received from Leonard saying he was interested in the idea of dual personalities, or people's view of themselves versus how they are seen by the world. In his previous photographic series, *Shekhina* and *The Full Body Project*, he had very definite ideas of what he wanted to bring to the table as he posed and molded his subjects. But what if Leonard allowed the subjects to direct their own images? To show the side of themselves that no one knew, or perhaps the half of themselves they were searching for. "I'm particularly looking for people to surprise me and possibly themselves," he wrote. "To reveal a secret self. I'd like to ask them, 'Who do think you are?'"

To find out, we turned an area below the gallery into a waiting room and photography studio, and invited 100 people to participate over a three-day period. At first I thought I would just call on friends, but many of my friends are artists and writers, and it became apparent that the project would be more interesting if we were to get a wider cross-section of the social strata, and include people who are perhaps less comfortable revealing themselves than many artists.

I emailed a letter to some acquaintances, and clients, and friends of friends — I wanted businessmen and bus drivers, social workers and house-husbands, clergy and those in their congregation. (Interestingly, the only profession with a 100% refusal rate — four out of four — was bank president, all of whom answered in similar fashion: "My secret self is just as dull and uninteresting as my public self.").

A reporter heard about the project, and printed a short piece in the local paper. My in-box was inundated with volunteers, and everyone had comments and questions, both soul-searching and humorous:

I was wondering if Mr. Nimoy is looking more for an expression of the self that we keep hidden from others, or of the self that we would really like to be?

Shall we come in costume — like a Frieda Kahlo painting? Must I be nude? Can I paint Hebrew letters on my boobs?

Thank you very much for including the Mayor in this invitation. She considers it an honor to be asked to participate.

I eat MAJOR chocolate when no one's looking. Does something like this count?

Weird project, this. Sign me up.

What an interesting question to ponder. Who am I? Does Mr. Nimoy have any more concrete instructions for discovering that secret self?

Leonard's instructions were minimal. "The 'self we keep hidden from others and 'the self we would really like to be' might be one and the same," he suggested. "I leave it to the subjects to decide what they want to show to the camera. I hope the title is open enough to encourage broad interpretation."

Time slots were assigned, and subjects arrived. My daughter drove up from New York City to help check in everyone, and my wife stood in front of the gallery and convinced a few passersby to take a half hour out of their day and reveal their inner selves, so we would have a "control group" of random subjects. In the studio three assistants helped with the lights, the recording, and the computers. (For those interested in technical details, *Secret Selves* was shot with a Hasselblad H3D digital camera with 28mm, 80mm and 120mm lenses, Sekonic L508 light meter, Apple Macbook Pro laptop computer and additional calibrated LaCie 319LCD monitor for viewing images, although most of Leonard's earlier work is shot with film.) Leonard's wife, Susan, helped enormously with suggested poses, and insight into how best to draw out the story the model was trying to tell.

As each subject walked into the studio, some eagerly, most nervously, Leonard approached each for a short conversation. The goal was to put them at ease, find out their "real life" identity, and what inner self they hoped Leonard might capture. At the last moment, we decided to video the proceedings, more as a method of archival documentation than with the idea of expanding the project. But it became apparent immediately that these exchanges were illuminating and would have a greater role in the final exhibit than anticipated. Within a few minutes, Leonard was able to bring the subjects deeper inside their own self than they had intended to travel. What began as a lark for many turned into a truly revealing and emotional experience. And at just the moment they were most themselves — and often off-guard — the shutter snapped. And snapped again.

Why were so many willing to take time out of their busy schedules to take part in this project? I polled people on their way in to the shoot, and the answer almost always had to do with their appreciation of Mr. Nimoy's artistic career. But the conversation on the way out was much different. If they had come to meet the personality, they left transformed, discussing the art and the artist, the man who had brought out their secret selves and, with his craft and vision, captured it at a moment in time.

— Richard Michelson, R. Michelson Galleries, Northampton, Massachusetts

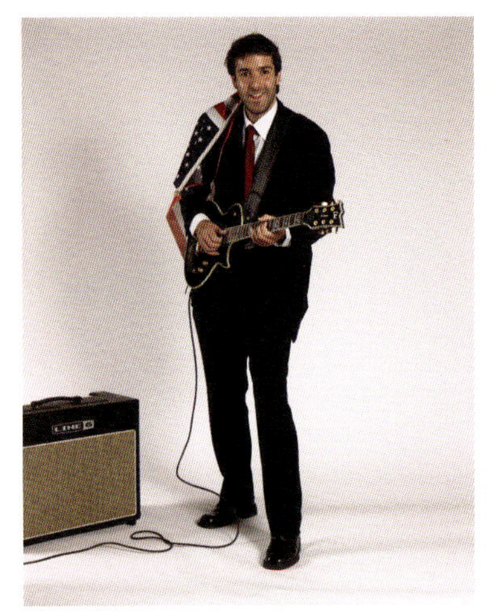

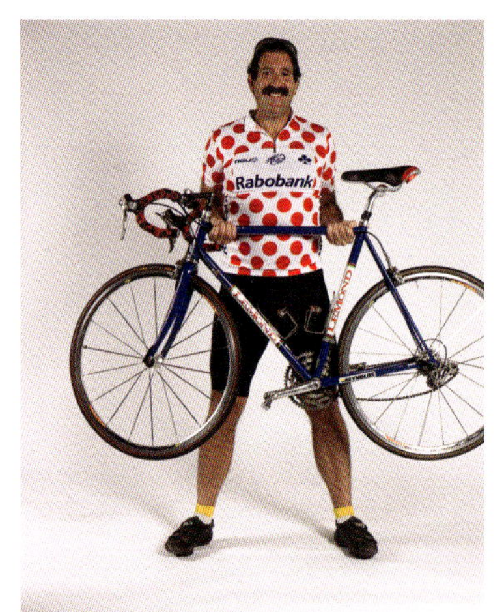
Rabobank

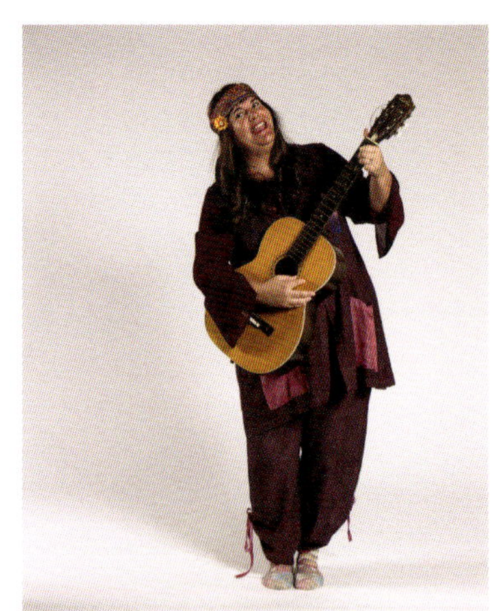

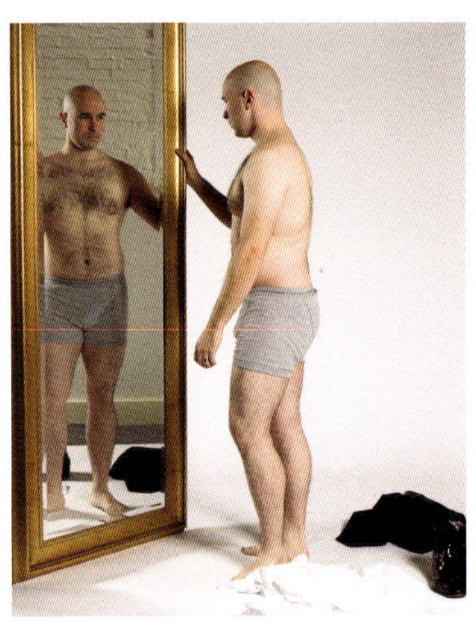

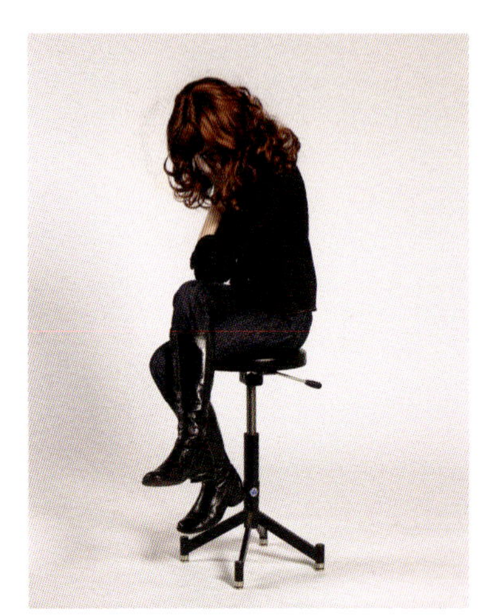

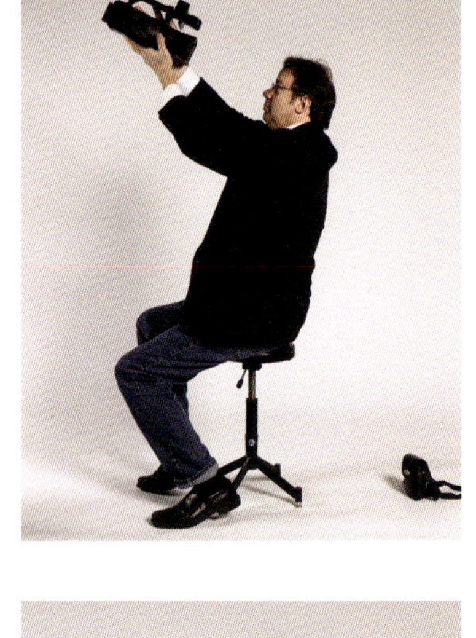

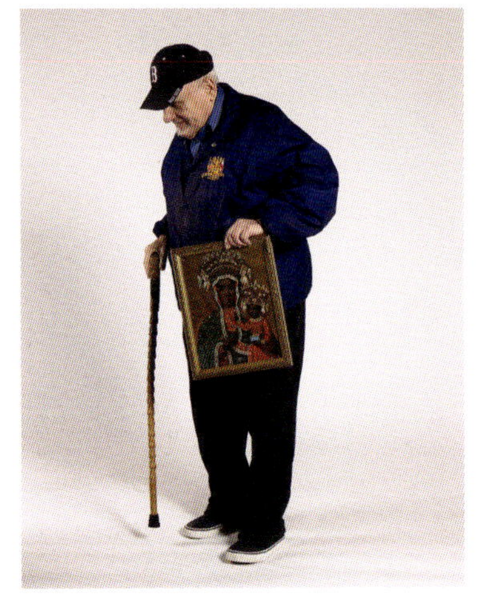

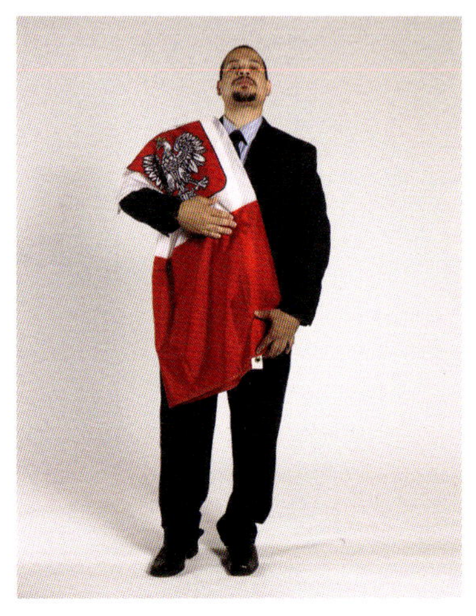

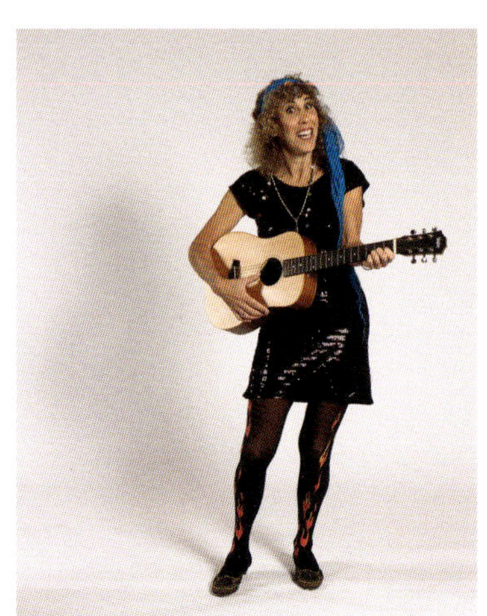

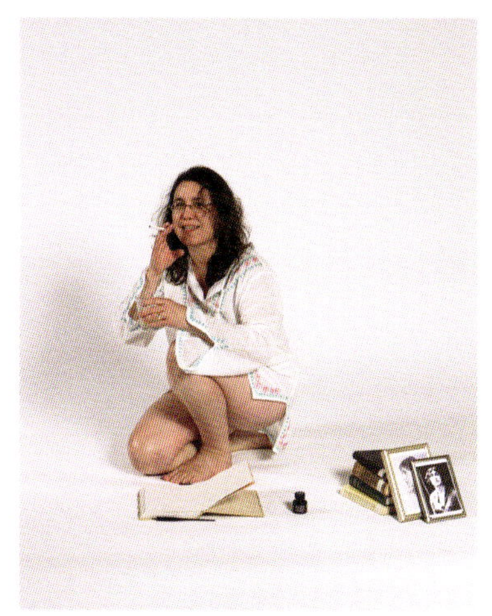
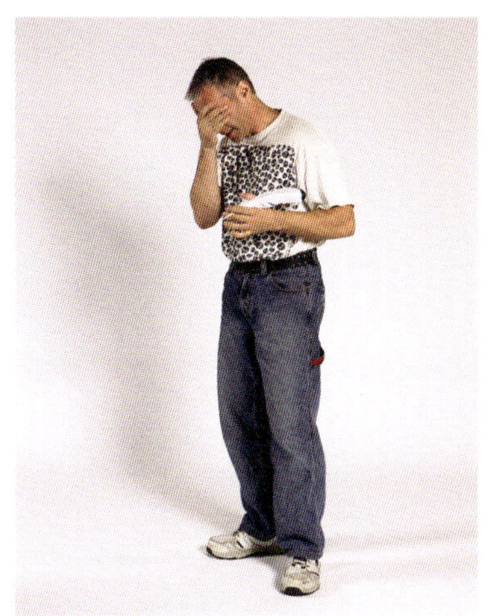
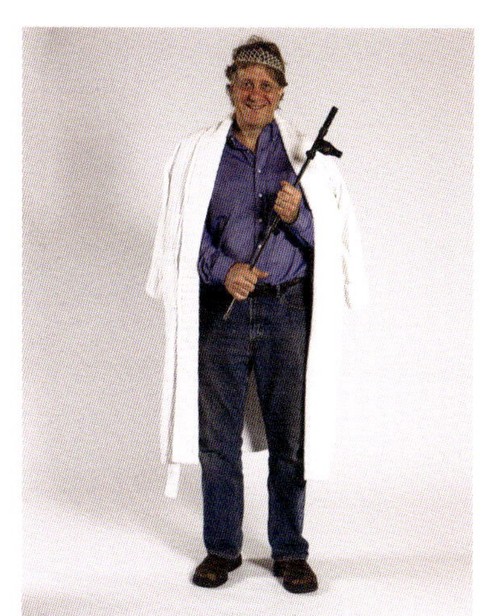
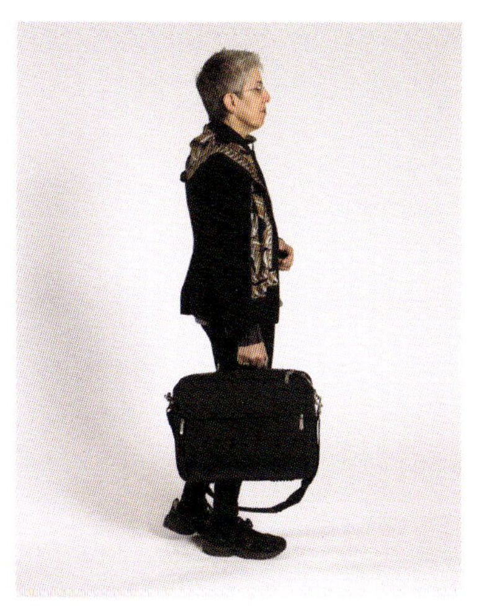
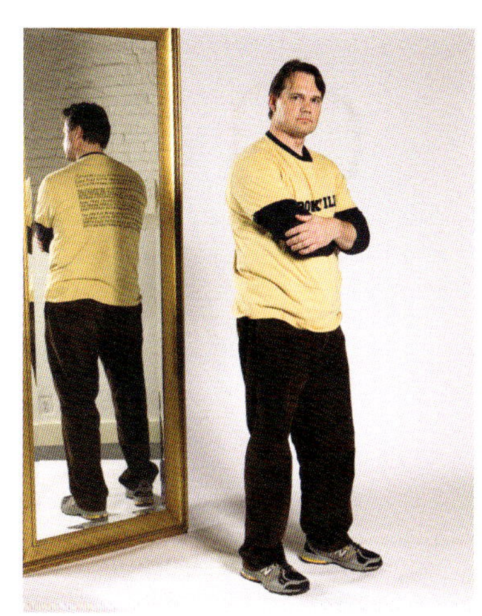
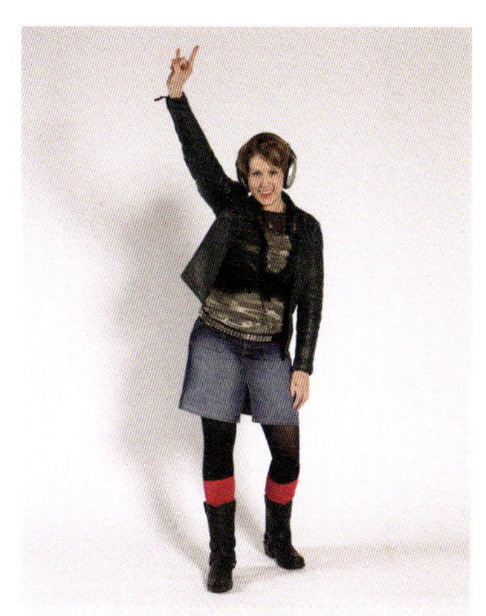
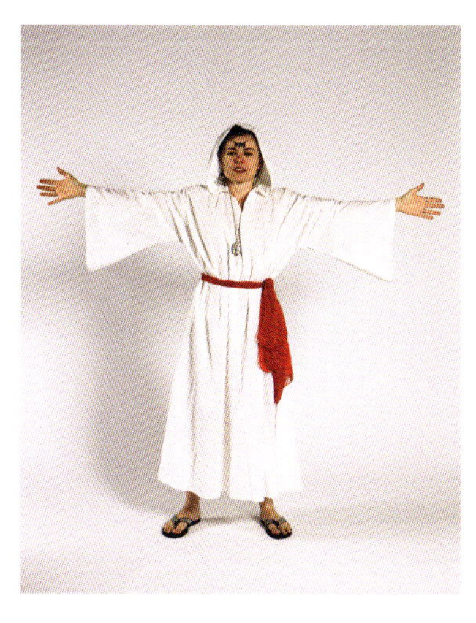
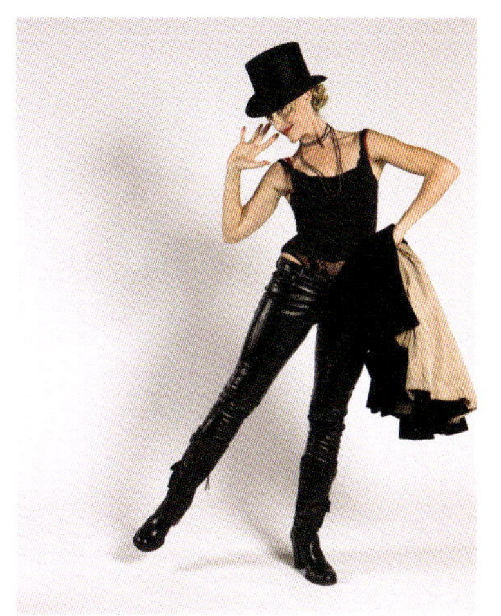
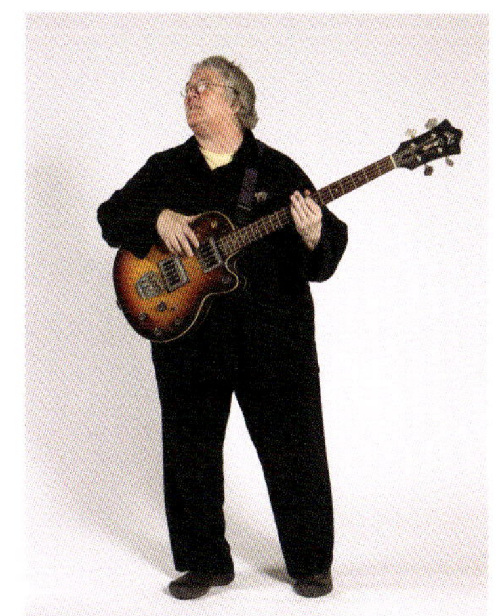

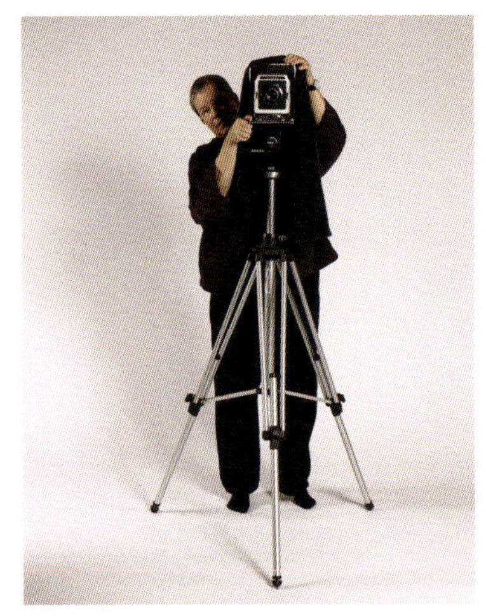
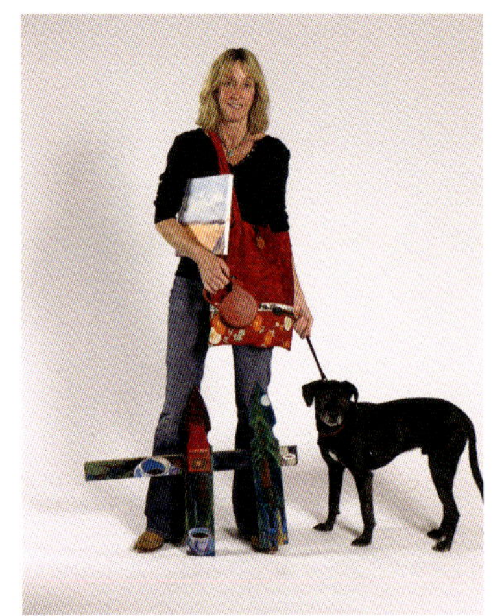
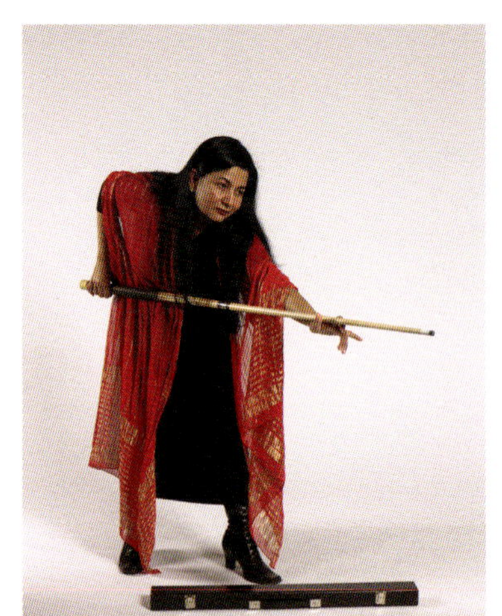
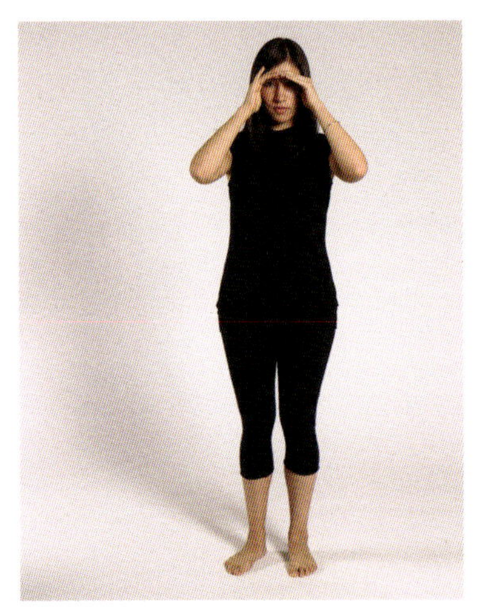
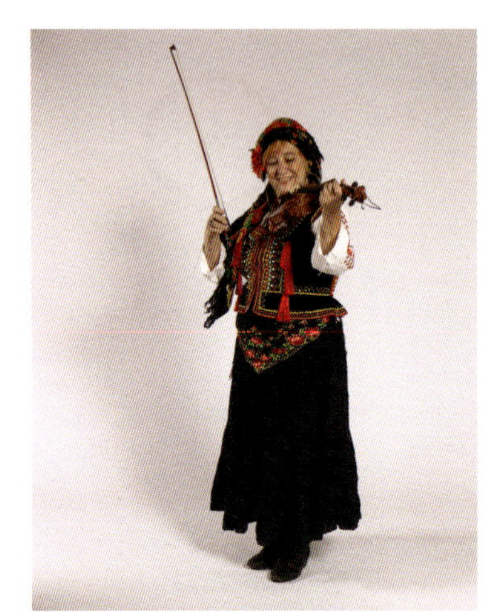
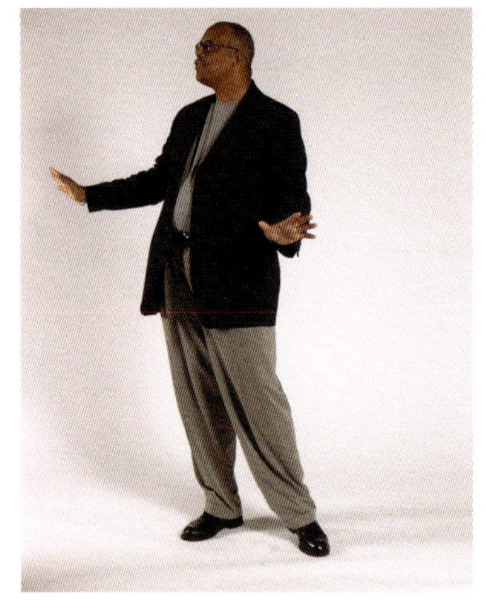
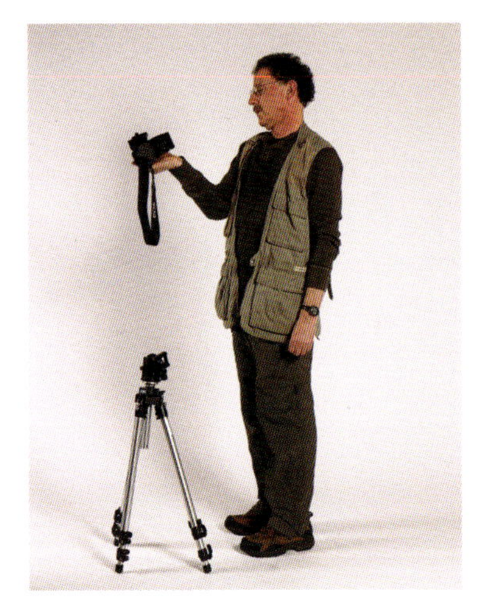
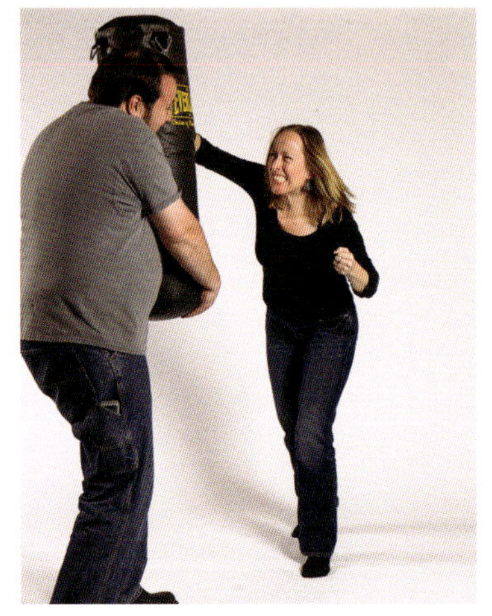
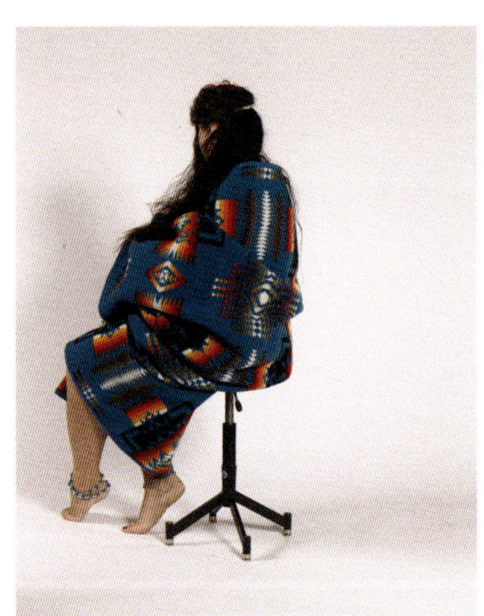

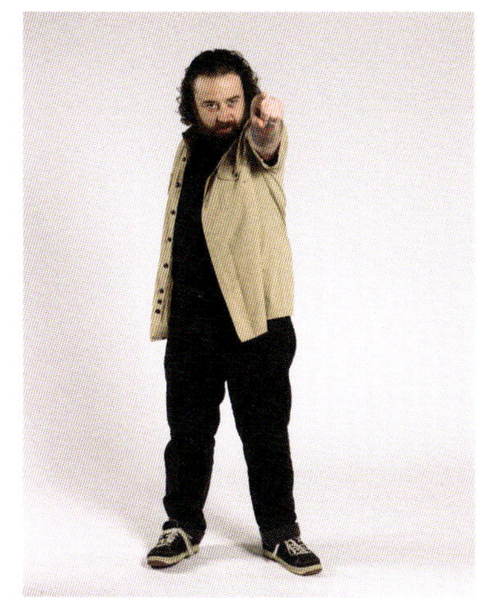
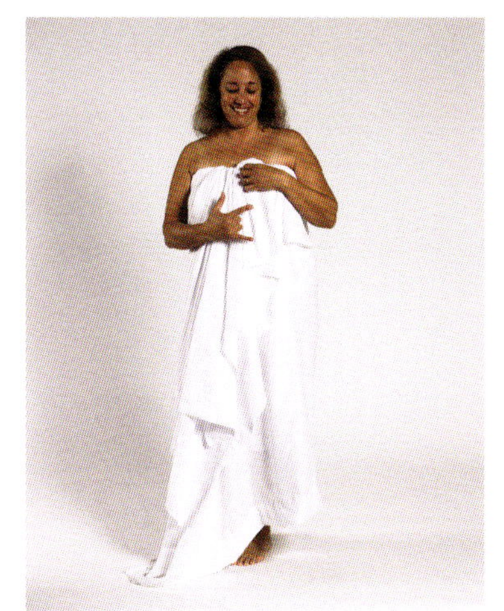
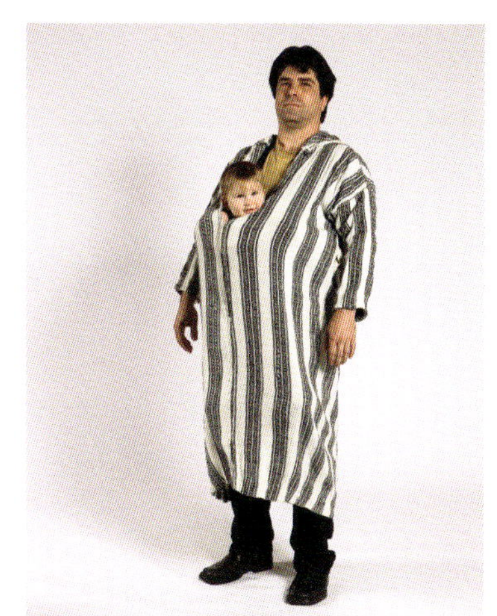
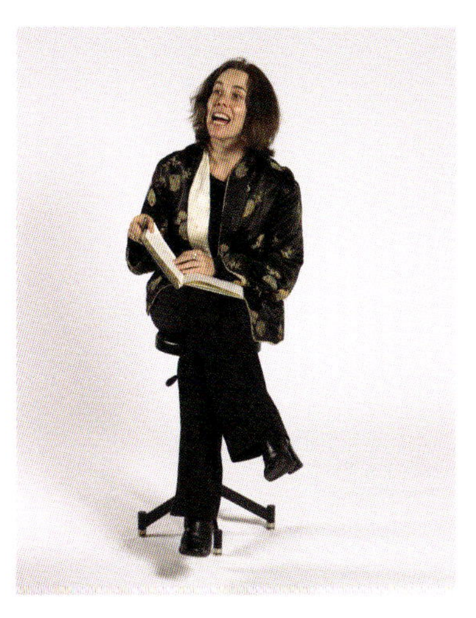
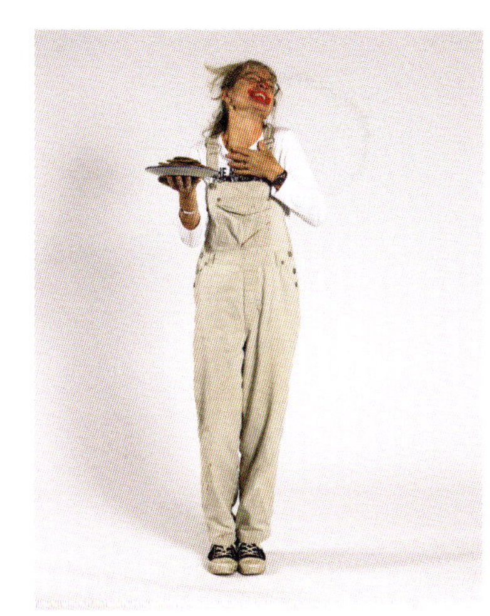
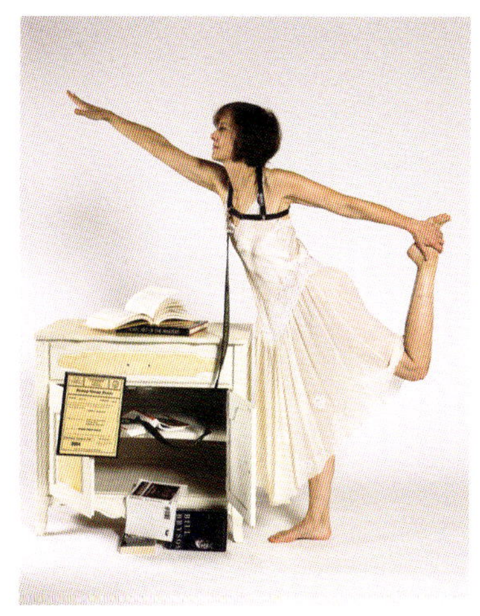
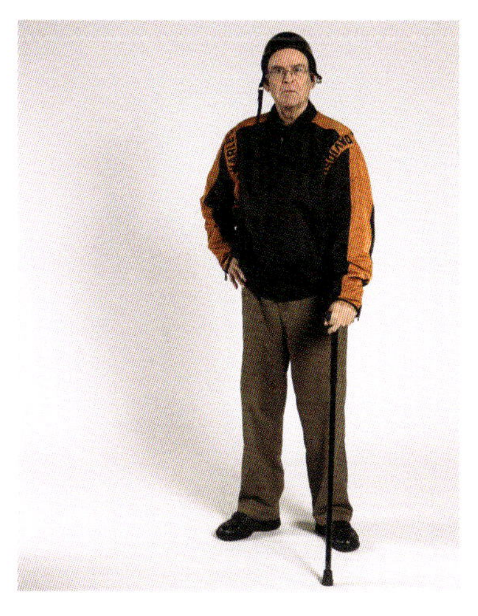
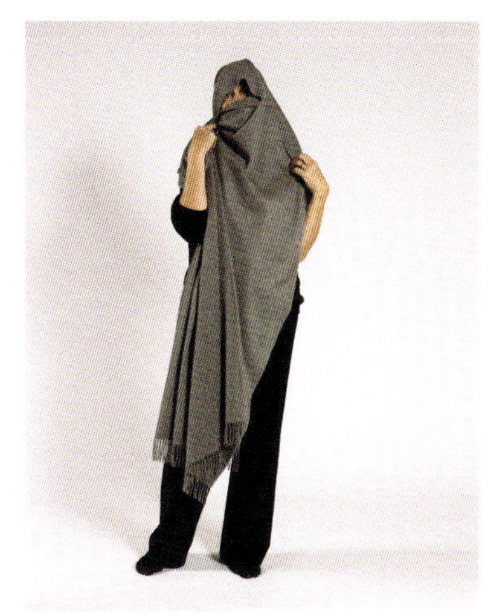
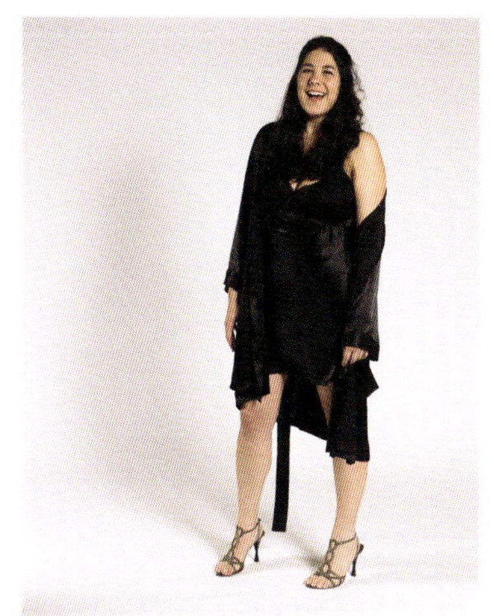

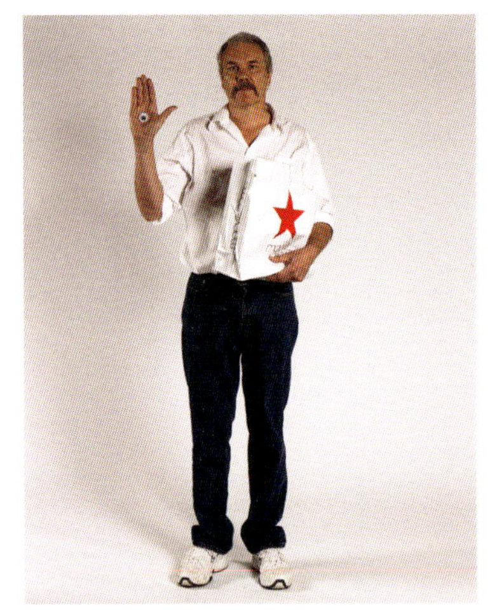
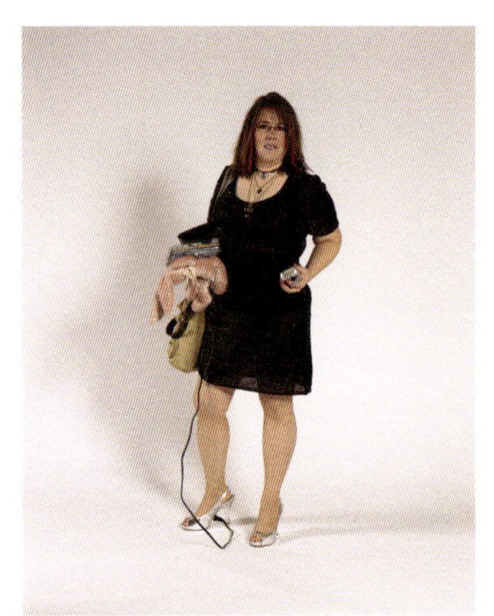
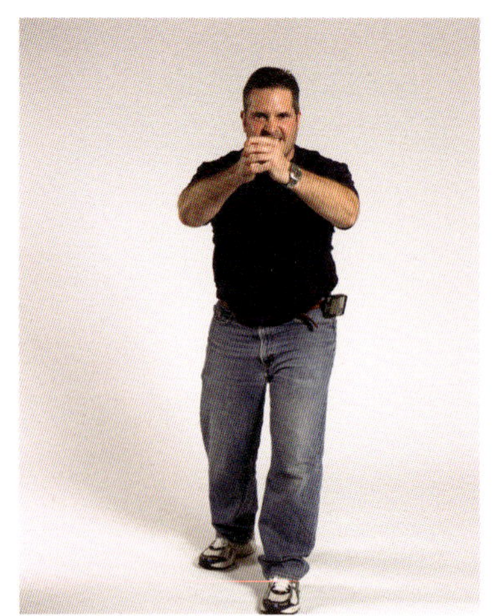
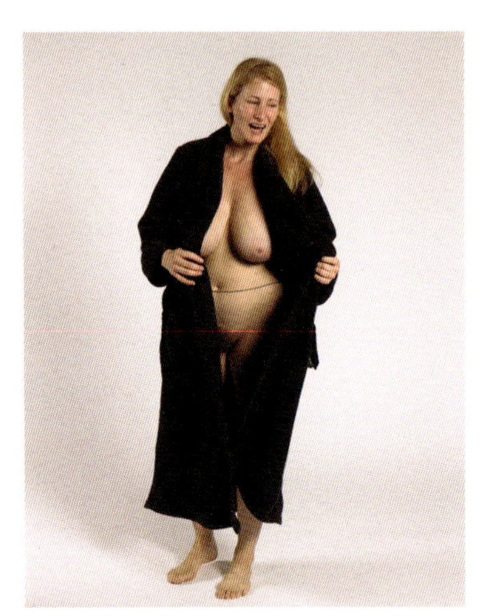
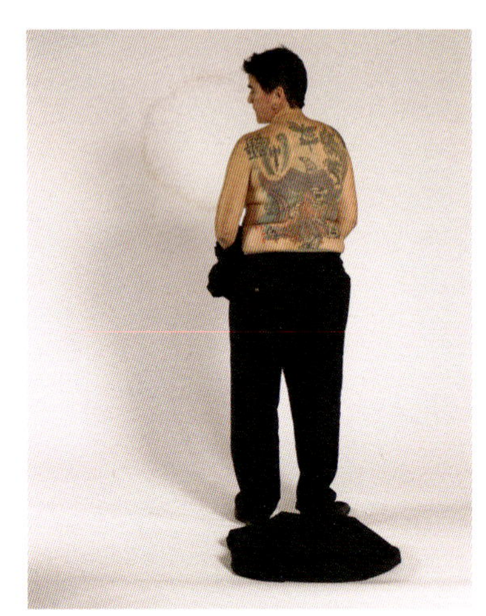
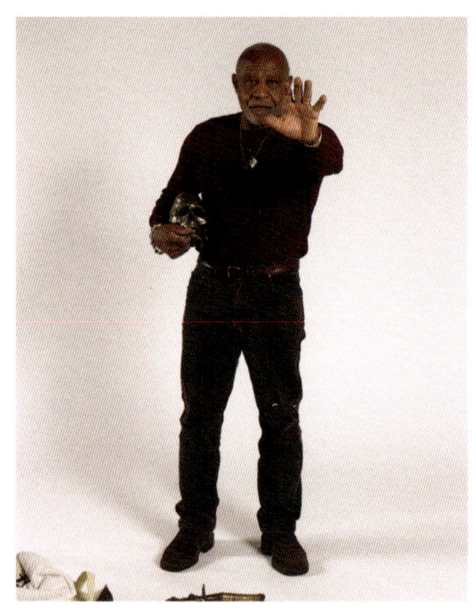
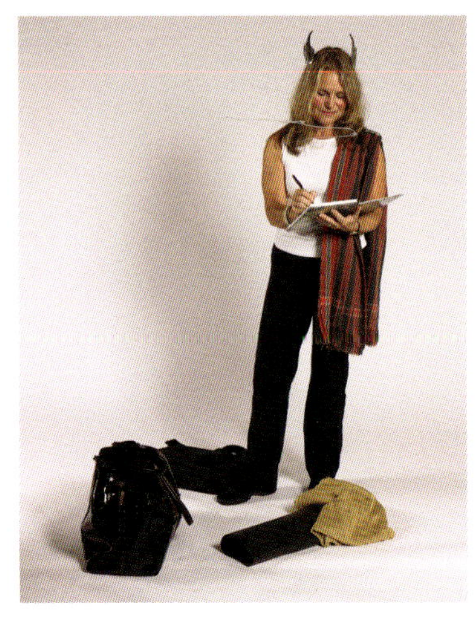
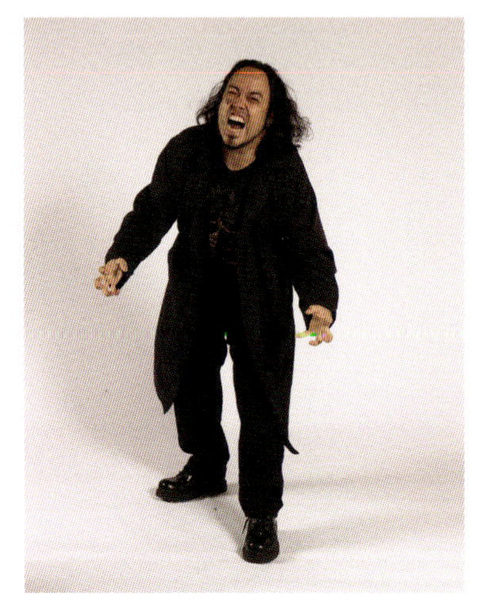
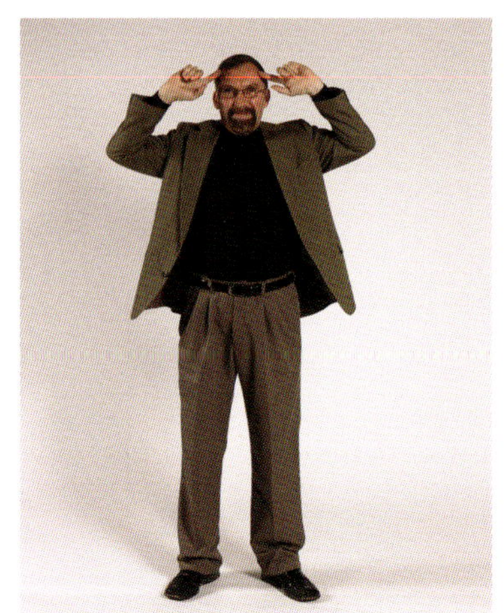

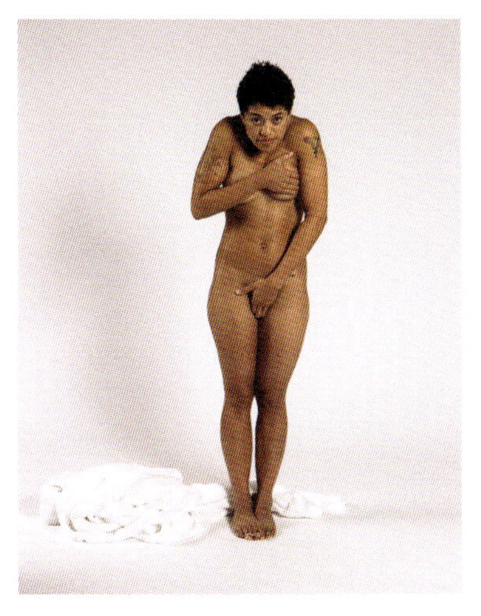
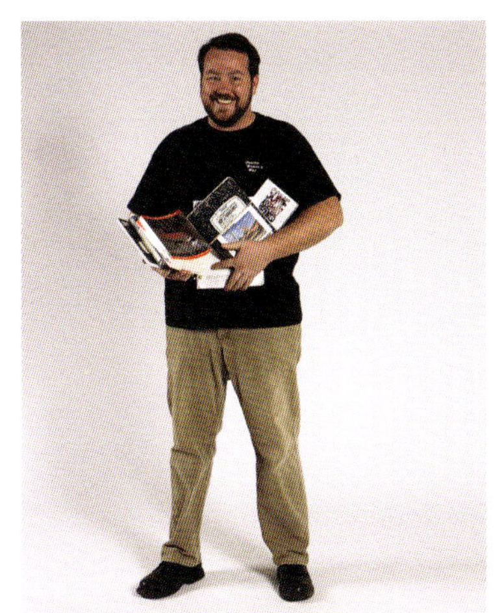
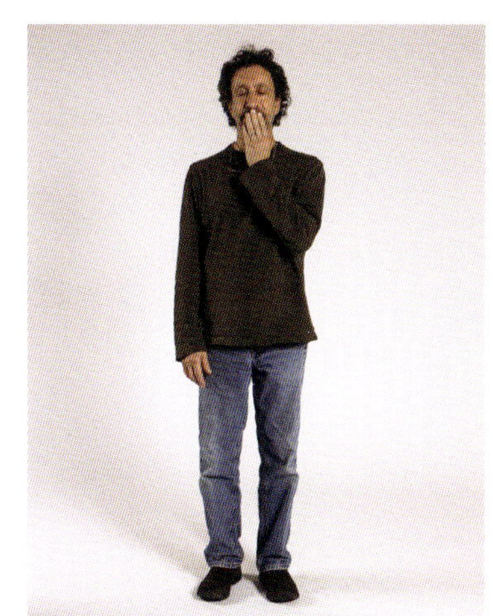
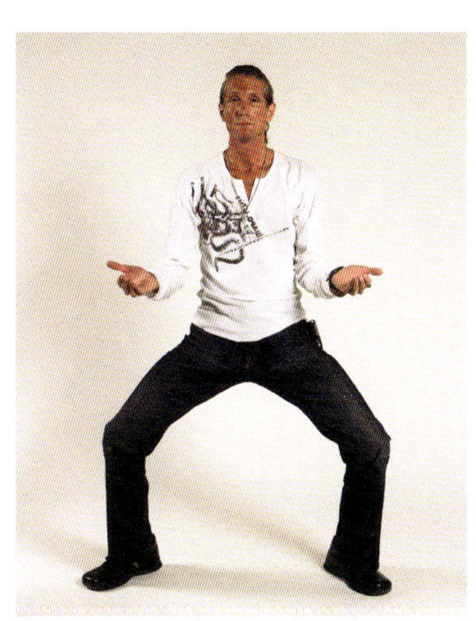
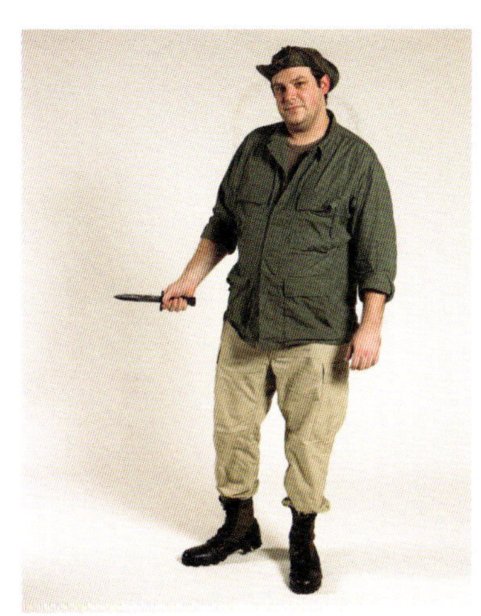
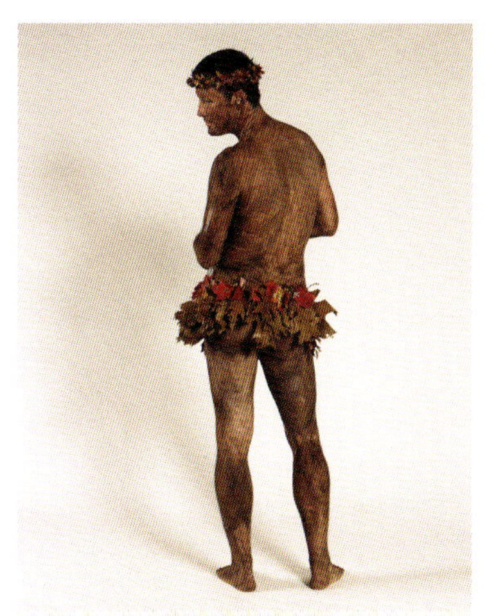
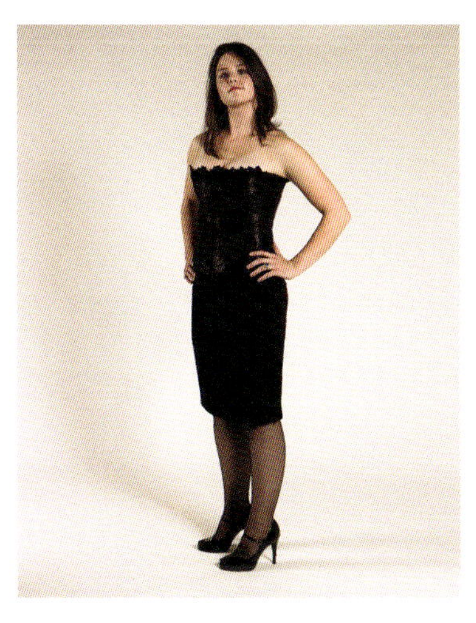
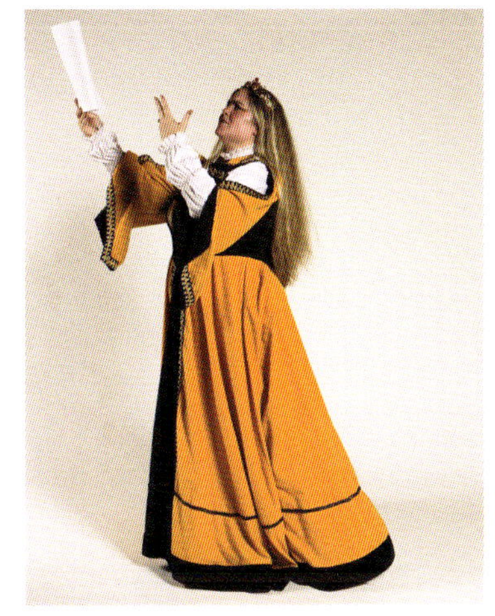
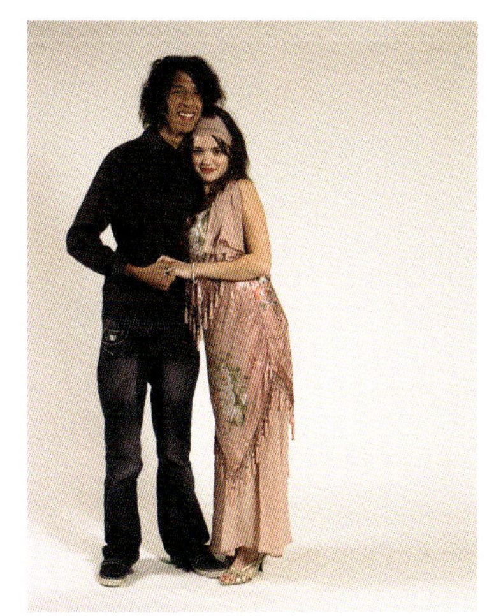

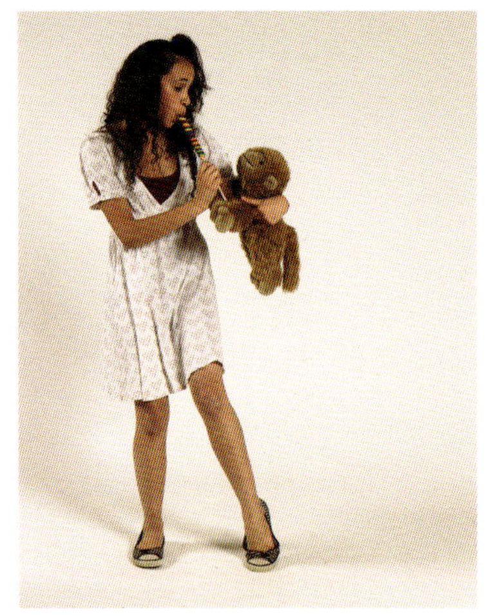
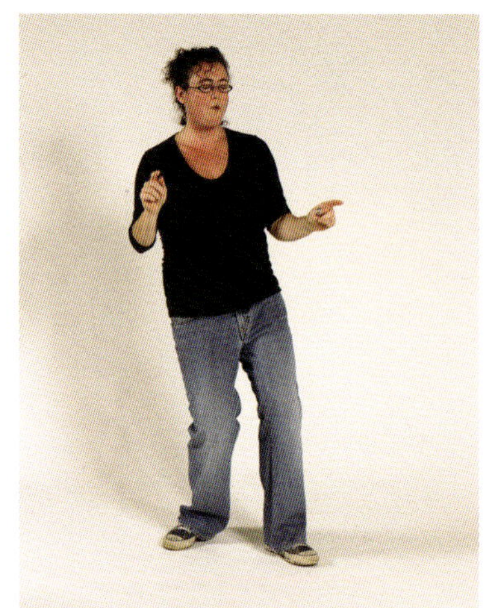
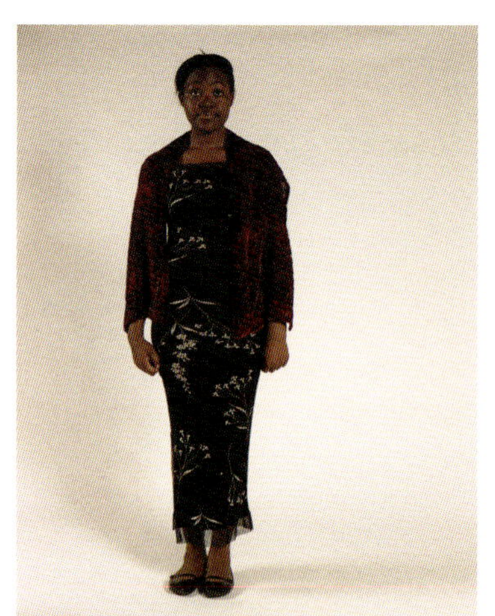
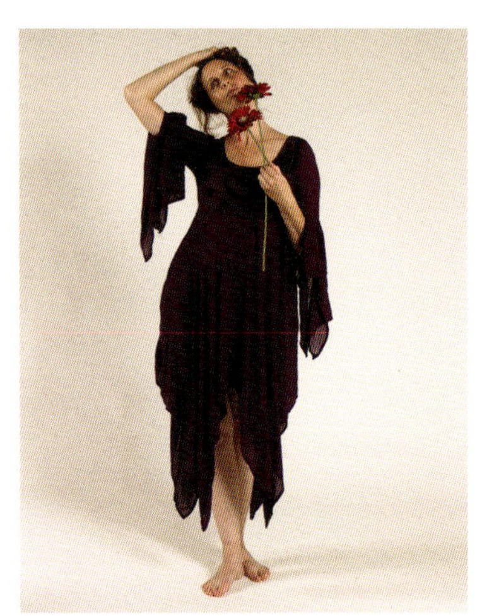
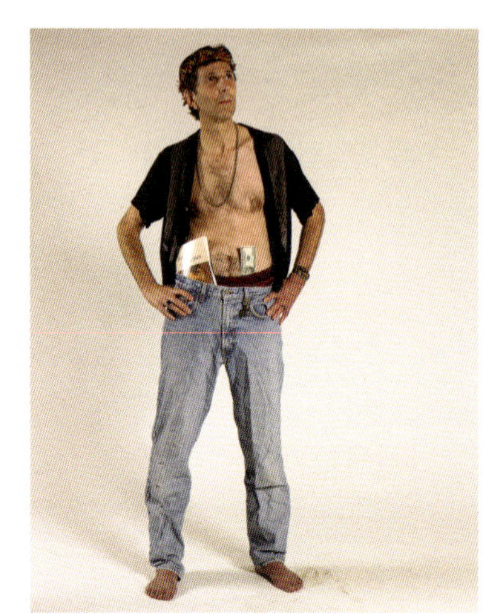
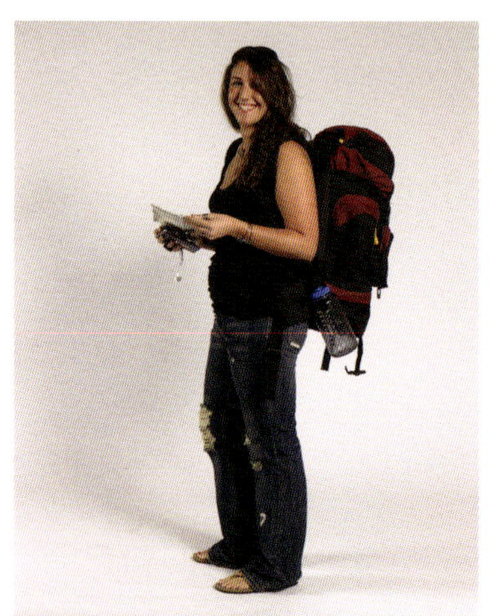
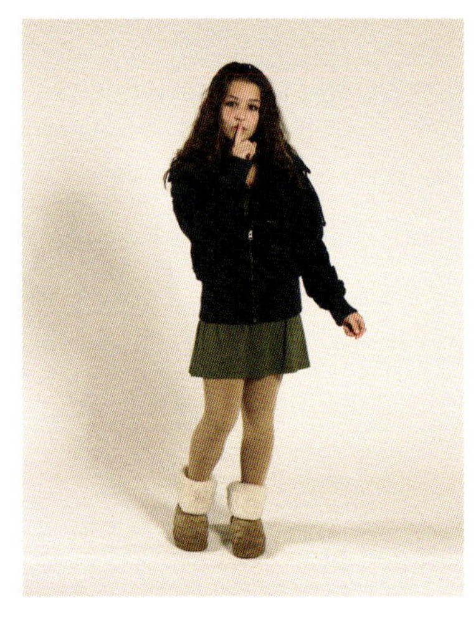
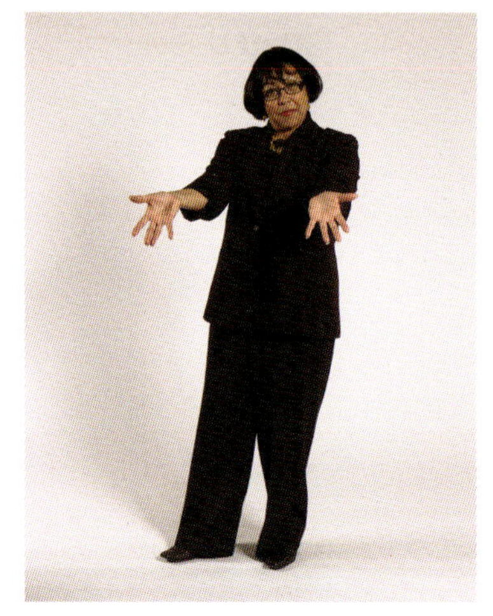
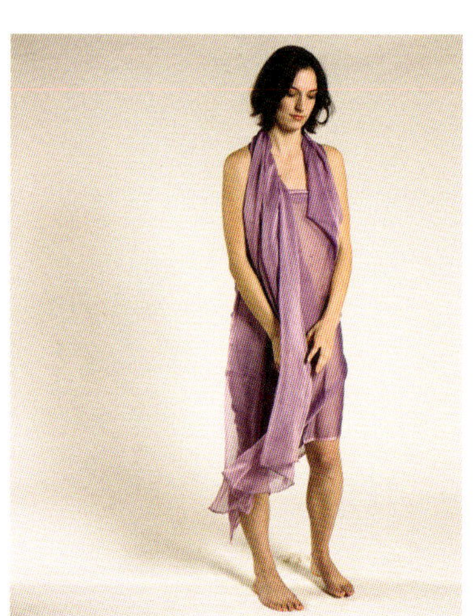

The real me is the one who is not worthy. ▪ *If I weren't the mayor I'd be singing.* ▪ *My Secret Self is the "Courageous Alpha Male." My public self is very Beta.* ▪ *I am an amalgamation of Aphrodite (love) and Isis (wife/mother).* ▪ *My secret self is a running commentary interrupted by memory.* ▪ *My stronger façade sometimes fails, but every once in a while the clouds part and, I am full and in balance.* ▪ *I am still the shy one who stuttered until I was 25.* ▪ *I would like to be invisible.* ▪ *I am consistently inconsistent. I crave stability but hide from commitment.* ▪ *My secret self would love to be that lost sensual woman I forget I can be.* ▪ *I am dark, defiant and devoid of responsibility. The complete opposite of the real me.* ▪ *My other self looks to the fourth dimension, where the unseen is real.* ▪ *If I have a secret life, then it involves the grief I bear for the living loss of one of my children.* ▪ *I have a secret desire to be a vigilante lunatic like "The Punisher."* ▪ *My secret self yearns for time to just express my artistic side without the fear of conscience.* ▪ *Who am I really? I don't know but when I dance I am confident and comfortable.* ▪ *My secret self is a mad, passionate lover who ravishes his woman sensually in public displays of affection.* ▪ *Society tells me to hold my breath, nature tells me to breathe!* ▪ *I desire to be someone who embodies feminine sexuality but is afraid to.* ▪ *Here I can wear pink. My real self rarely does.* ▪ *I would like to see how it would be to be rich.*

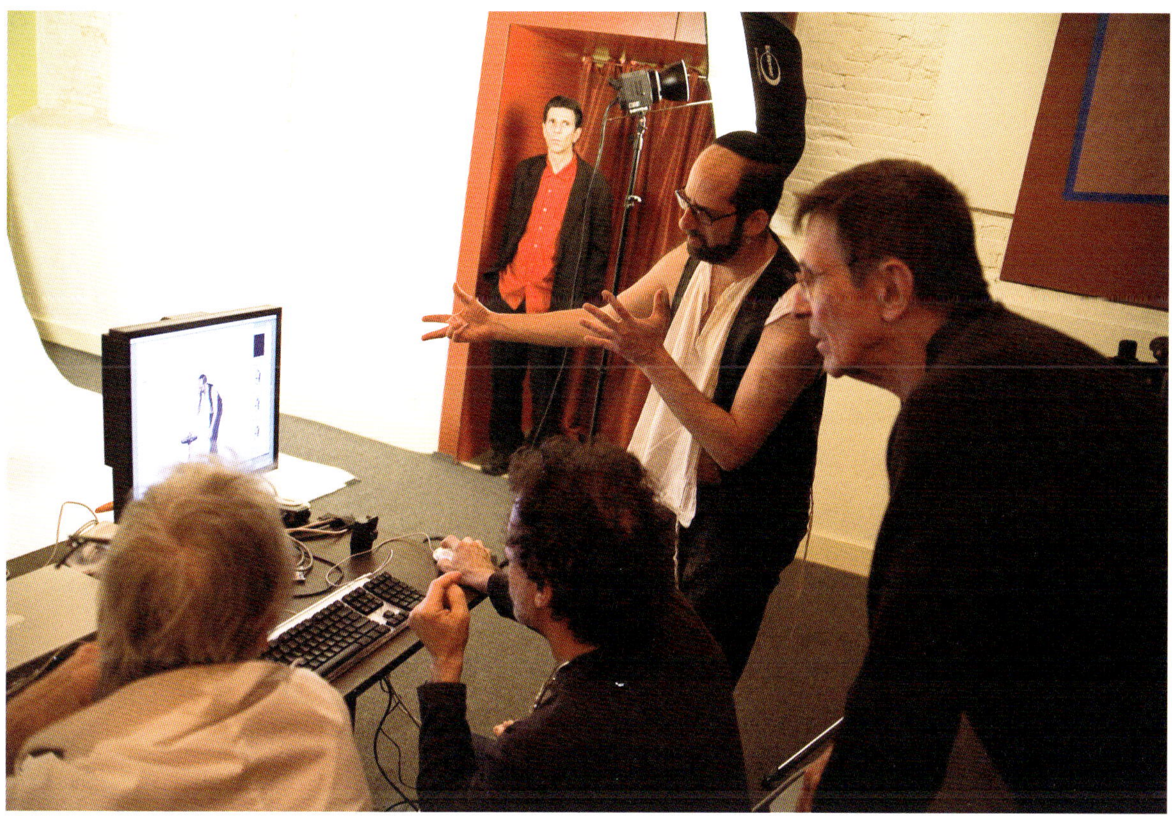

SPONSORS

We are grateful for the generous support of Bonnie Moss. In addition, we'd like to thank our sponsors: Sloane Aubrey, Wyatt Aubrey, Ella Baff, Rachel Barenblat, Anna Beischer, Lily Beischer, Thomas Beischer, Zach Beischer, Catherine E. Bell, Joan Benjamin, Joyce Bernstein, Lisa M. Blackmer, William C. Blackmer, Jr., Representative Dan Bosley, Jane Braus, Cameron Brown, Duncan Brown, Isa Brown, Kienan Brown, Quinn Brown, Susan Brown, Jeremy Brown-Adams, Walker Brown-Adams, Andrew Bruun, Elisif Bruun, Elizabeth Bruun, Kayla Bruun, Rebecca Bruun, Sophia Bruun, Justin Bucksbaum, Marissa E. Carlson, Larry Cherkis, Donna Consolini, Paula Consolini, Liliana Crewdson, Walker Crewdson, Milo Crosby, Player Crosby, Bob Doran, Happy Doran, Jane Eckert, Mark Edelstein & Dr. Pat Barbanell, Patty & Joel Ellis, Shirley & Manny Finkelstein, Susan Fox, Jennifer Frutchy, Danny Gold, David Gold, John Gold, Liz Gold, Susan Gold, Tom Gold, Deborah Grausman, Jennifer Grausman, Richard Grausman, Susan Grausman, Susan Green, Owen Gregoricus, Judy & Bruce Grinnell, Lisa Hamner, Georgia E. W. Hannock, Charlotte Hemr, Joseph Hemr, Kurt Hemr, Louisa Hemr, Lucy Holland, Bedloe Holton-Roth, Kenya Holton-Roth, The Hoopers, Molly Howard, Noah Howard, Sally Kramarsky, Wynn Kramarsky, Fran Lapidus, Ira Lapidus, Ailish Learsy, Ezra Learsy-Cahill, Otto Learsy-Cahill, Ava Sutton Leonardo, Gary Leopold, Carol A. LeWitt, Eva LeWitt, Sofia LeWitt, Leigh Missaggia, Jeremy Mittleman, Nora Mittleman, Alexander Starr Nader, Antara Sage Nader, Sasha Belle Nader, Kenneth Nash, Suzanne Nash, Ellen & George Needham and family, Laura Overstreet, Vincent C. Paladino, Deborah A. Pege, Cole Peppis, Tess Peppis, Bobbie Reno, Jock Reynolds, Isaac Rosenthal, Lawrence Rosenthal, Joan & Michael Salke, Elizabeth G. Sanzone, Martin Scanlan, Stella Scanlan, Gregory Scheckler, Eric Schrauwen, Charlie Schulze, Oliver W. Schulze, Theodore M. Schulze, Warren Schwartz, Sundae Shields, Emma Stegeman, Rosa Stegeman, Sheila M. Stone, Fiona Tarses, Harry Tarses, Larkin Tarses, Nelson Tarses, Pippa Tarses, Tess Tarses, Chad Wadsworth, Jack Wadsworth, Kevin Wadsworth, Oscar Wadsworth, Robyn Wadsworth, Spencer Wadsworth, Susy Wadsworth, Wiley Wadsworth, Claudia Y.C. Wair, W. Ligaya Ward, Tom & Suky Werman, Noah Wertheimer, Rebecca Wertheimer, The Williams Inn, Jeff Zeeman, Daniel Zilkha, Lucinda Zilkha, Michael Zilkha, Nina Zilkha, and anonymous.

COLOPHON

Published on the occasion of *Leonard Nimoy: Secret Selves* on view at MASS MoCA from July 31, 2010, through December 2010.

Published by
MASS MoCA
1040 MASS MoCA Way
North Adams, Massachusetts 01247-2450
413.MoCA.111
www.massmoca.org

Design by Dan McKinley
Printed by Kirkwood Printing in Massachusetts
ISBN: 0-9764276-9-9